SpringerBriefs in Law

SpringerBriefs present concise summaries of cutting-edge research and practical applications across a wide spectrum of fields. Featuring compact volumes of 50 to 125 pages, the series covers a range of content from professional to academic. Typical topics might include:

- A timely report of state-of-the art analytical techniques
- A bridge between new research results, as published in journal articles, and a contextual literature review
- A snapshot of a hot or emerging topic
- A presentation of core concepts that students must understand in order to make independent contributions

SpringerBriefs in Law showcase emerging theory, empirical research, and practical application in Law from a global author community. SpringerBriefs are characterized by fast, global electronic dissemination, standard publishing contracts, standardized manuscript preparation and formatting guidelines, and expedited production schedules.

Bede Harris

Cultivating Good Citizenship

Civics Education, Constitutional Structures and Political Leadership

Springer

Bede Harris
School of Business
Charles Sturt University
Albury, NSW, Australia

ISSN 2192-855X ISSN 2192-8568 (electronic)
SpringerBriefs in Law
ISBN 978-981-92-2739-6 ISBN 978-981-92-2740-2 (eBook)
https://doi.org/10.1007/978-981-92-2740-2

This Springer imprint is published by the registered company Springer Nature Singapore Pte Ltd.
The registered company address is: 152 Beach Road, #21-01/04 Gateway East, Singapore 189721, Singapore

This book is dedicated to my wife, Veronica, and to my daughter, Lizzie and to Buttons, Adeline, Floki, Cornelia and Hildegard who watched as I wrote it.

Preface

This book deals with the idea of citizenship, not in the sense of a statutory regime that regulates a person's right to live and exercise political rights in a particular jurisdiction, but rather in the sense of the values and practices that should underlie a person's conduct as a member of society. This concept of citizenship is therefore relevant both to people who hold the formal status of citizenship and those who do not. The importance of citizenship in this broad sense is self-evident: a society in which people behave ethically towards each other, both in the conduct of politics and in their inter-personal relationships, will be healthier than one in which they do not. The need to cultivate good citizenship has become all the more urgent in light of current assaults on reason as the foundation of debate, growing intolerance of opposing views and a coarsening in political behaviour, all of which have led to a decline in public confidence in government, resulting in many becoming disillusioned with, and disengaged from, public affairs, which further weakens the political system.

Although there is much in this book that relates to law—in particular the constitutional mechanisms necessary for citizenship to flourish—the book is only incidentally about law and is principally about values. The relationship between law and values is often misunderstood: Whereas law creates rules, it is a truism to say that it cannot create values, as these are internal to each human being. Indeed, law itself reflects the values underlying society. It follows that the ethical quality of the law depends on the ethical quality of a society's values. This is why deciding what those values are is a step that must be taken prior to the establishing the legal order. Prime examples of where this was done were the drafting of constitutions in Germany after World War 2 and in South Africa after the demise of apartheid. In both instances, the constitution expressly stated that it was based on the value of human dignity and required the courts to interpret the constitution—and therefore the validity of law—in accordance with that value.

However, it is only infrequently that societies find themselves in circumstances where an entirely new constitutional order needs to be adopted, but even where an existing constitution remains in force, the question of what values should underly the constitution must be addressed in order to ensure the ethical content of the law made under its authority. Unfortunately, few governments initiate such a process of introspection, with the result that existing values continue to shape the law. This has negative consequences even in democracies, because in the absence of a values-based constitutional restraint on law-making powers, the result is that the law is shaped by whatever values—and prejudices—happen to be shared by passing majorities. Of course, majorities are entitled to act in accordance with their self-interest when exercising their power to elect legislators, but unless there is some limit on what law can be made on their behalf, there is nothing to protect individuals and minorities from being subject to majoritarian tyranny. In short, a society where people lack good values will be one in which bad governments will be elected and bad law enacted. While it is understandable that, when constitutional lawyers evaluate whether a country has good government, they focus on how its institutions are designed—and that is undoubtedly important—far more determinative of the quality of government in a country is the ethical character of its citizens.

How does one determine which are the good values that citizens should uphold? How goodness is defined is a broad philosophical question that will perpetually engage us, but an attempt must be made to answer it if we are to reach any conclusions about what constitutes good citizenship. This book draws upon ancient Greek and Roman political philosophy, Enlightenment ideas relating to human autonomy, post-World War 2 human rights declarations and John Rawls' technique for the objective determination of rules, to define goodness as respect for human dignity as the fundamental value, and argues that good citizenship requires a person to act in accordance with that value.

How are respect for human dignity and the practice of good citizenship to be cultivated? The obvious answer is by means of education, but unfortunately education systems are notoriously bad at teaching values. This is reflected in the fact that civics and citizenship, which are two distinct bodies of knowledge, are often conflated. Yet the difference between them is crucial in appreciating what an education system should provide. Civics is the study of the institutions of government and how they interact. Citizenship is the study of values according to which the citizen acts. In most countries, education systems focus almost exclusively on the former, even if both are referred to in the names of programmes of study. The result is that—at best—those countries produce young people who understand the mechanics of government, but have no understanding of values, and have not had cultivated in them the intellectual capacity to make the ethical judgements required of a citizen. There is therefore little wonder that societies where citizens make decisions based on no value other than self-interest produce politicians who similarly prioritise self-interest, and whose conduct in government leads to citizens becoming disillusioned with, and therefore disengaged from, political processes.

Being a good citizen is difficult. It requires a willingness to shoulder the burdens of continuing self-education and active participation in public affairs. It also requires the practice of the virtues of reason, tolerance and empathy. Under the broad view of citizenship adopted in this book, these practices should guide behaviour not only in the political sphere but also in day-to-day interactions—in other words, being a good citizen means being not only an ethical political actor but also an ethical person. In this sense, good citizenship provides a set of secular values to guide society in place of religious values which, being based on faith, are obviously unsuited to a society where decisions are (or should be) based on reason, where there is a wide variety of religions each with their own (often conflicting) value systems and where there are also people who adhere to no religion.

A citizen's capacity to engage in public life depends on the institutional framework within which politics is conducted—the desire to act as a good citizen cannot be fulfilled, at least in so far as the political dimension of citizenship is concerned, unless the freedom to do so exists. This requires that a country's constitution contain a bill of rights that protects the freedoms implied by human dignity and provides remedies that can be granted by an independent judiciary in cases of breach. Also important to the exercise of citizenship are structural aspects of a country's legal system, including an electoral system that ensures not only that each person has a vote but also that, as far as possible, each vote has equal effect on the composition of the legislature, and that there are mechanisms that ensure executive accountability.

Although the freedom to further one's own interests when engaging in politics either as voter or politician is a key element of the exercise of citizenship, good citizenship may require that a person act against their own interests when the public good requires it. This echoes the Roman concept of civic republicanism in terms of which citizenship was held to confer rights of political participation but also the duty to exercise such rights not solely for personal benefit but also for the public good. These two strands—individual and communitarian—balanced each other and, if given equal value, have the effect of restraining political actors, be they voters or politicians, in the exercise of power. Unfortunately, current reality is that few politicians act in any way other than the furtherance of self-interest. In a democracy, voters bear ultimate responsibility for who governs them and so the fault is theirs if those they elect turn out to govern badly, which highlights the importance of citizens being exposed to values-based civics education.

The most important consequence of this book for me as a constitutional lawyer has been to understand the limits of the law: Law is a coercive system and also an *ex post facto* one. Its power is felt after it has been breached and a sanction is imposed as a consequence. The law does not make people good—it merely acts as an externally-imposed deterrent against bad conduct. By contrast, good citizenship is founded on a voluntary commitment to behave in accordance with ethical concern for one's fellow human beings. Voters and the leaders they elect cannot be mandated to practise the civic virtues of reason, tolerance, participation and kindness – these must become internalised dispositions of character cultivated through education. In an age of a decrease in trust in democracy, and an increase in alienation and disconnection from politics, the need to do this becomes all the more pressing.

Albury, Australia
March 2026

Bede Harris

Acknowledgements

I would like to acknowledge the assistance provided by the Faculty of Business, Justice and Behavioural Studies at Charles Sturt University for giving me sabbatical leave to enable me to write this book and who generously gave me a grant that enabled me to conduct a survey of levels of knowledge of civics and attitudes to constitutional reform in Australia. I would also like to acknowledge the assistance provided by library staff at the Albury and Bathurst campuses of Charles Sturt University, and in particular the prompt way in which they filled my many requests for inter-library loans. I would like to acknowledge Mamun Mishra, Karthikeyan Krishnan, Cynthia Kroonen and Nobuko Kamikawa at Springer Nature who oversaw the project at its various stages.

Contents

About the Author

Bede Harris was born in Zimbabwe. After graduating with a BA(Mod) from Trinity College, University of Dublin, he studied law in South Africa and graduated with an LLB from Rhodes University. He began his academic career at the University of Natal, Pietermaritzburg. He subsequently taught at the University of Waikato in New Zealand, where he obtained his DPhil. He was awarded a Fulbright Senior Scholarship and attended the American Studies Institute at Lafayette College in the United States. He is a Senior Lecturer in Law at Charles Sturt University and is the author of eight previous books and over 60 book chapters and articles on constitutional law, human rights, Indigenous legal issues, corporations law and consumer law.

Chapter 1
What is Good Citizenship?

Abstract This chapter discusses the idea of citizenship in the broad sense of the ethical and behavioural expectations of a person as a member of society, as distinct from the narrow legal sense of a set of rights that distinguishes a person from non-citizens. Its focus is on how to explain what is meant by 'good citizenship,' which leads to an inquiry into what is meant by 'good.' In answering this, the chapter examines the concept of virtue as understood in ancient Greece and Rome which, in the context of public life and according to the theory of civic republicanism adopted by Cicero and others, required respect both for individual rights and for communitarian obligations. The idea of virtue was founded upon natural law as ordained by the gods and was therefore ultimately dependant on faith. This is unsuitable as the foundational value for modern societies which are—or should be—governed by reason. Renaissance and Enlightenment philosophers developed a secular value system founded on the idea that each person was entitled to human dignity, which in turn entitled them to respect for their autonomy. In the twentieth century, respect for human dignity formed the basis for international human rights documents. The chapter ends with a discussion of how Rawls' concept of the veil of ignorance and his liberty and equality principles can be used to provide justification for a universal dignity-based value system.

1.1 What Does 'Good Citizenship' Mean?

To understand what is meant by 'good citizenship,' one first needs to understand the various meanings of the word 'citizenship' itself. The narrow legal meaning of citizenship refers to a legal status that a person has vis a vis the state, conferring various rights including political participation.[1] Citizenship in this sense has been described as[2]

---

[1] Heater (1999, p. 83).

[2] Humanity International (2009).

B. Harris, *Cultivating Good Citizenship*,
SpringerBriefs in Law, https://doi.org/10.1007/978-981-92-2740-2_1

> ...a status, corresponding to a collection of legal rights and serving as the foundation of political legitimacy in a democratic society, and an identity based on a sentiment of belonging to a political collective and a source of social linkage.

However, the concept of citizenship that is the subject of this book is far broader and refers to the relationship a person has to the rest of society, irrespective of whether they are citizens in the legal sense—what has been described as 'the quality of a person's response to membership in a community'.[3] Citizenship in this sense refers to the 'ethical ideals, behaviours and expectations of participation'[4] of a person as a member of society. Another definition which captures the breadth of the concept is that proposed by Skach who says that a citizen is 'a responsible, active member of the community called humanity, a member who enjoys rights but who also owes obedience to herself and to other humans.'[5]

Although people who are not citizens in the legal sense do not vote, they are not politically inert, and participate in politics albeit by informal means. So while many of the incidents of citizenship discussed in the book are relevant only to people who are citizens in the legal sense, others are relevant to non-citizen residents as well—an obvious example being the entitlement to human rights. This broad definition of citizenship is of particular importance to how people conduct themselves during the course of quotidian interactions with other members of the community.

The definition used in this book also highlights the fact that as areas of knowledge, 'civics' and 'citizenship,' although often conflated, are different. In this book the term 'civics' is used to refer to knowledge of the *mechanics* of government—about the institutions of the state, how they interact and the role of the citizen in that process. The term 'citizenship' is used to refer to the *values* required for good citizenship and the activities that give effect to them. The centrality of values to the concept of good citizenship was articulated in the summary of a survey of the views of teachers of citizenship in the United Kingdom, who defined good citizens as those who[6]

> ...conduct themselves in a strongly moral and ethical manner, who are very conscious of their community obligations, and who participate in the community in which they live.

Whether a person can be said to be a 'good citizen' depends on whether they conform to a set of norms. Therefore, unless one defines what one means by 'good,' one could say that a citizen who informs on political dissidents in a tyrannical society is as much a good citizen as one who protests against unlawful conduct by a public official in a free society. In each case, the citizen's conduct conforms to what is deemed good in that society. From this it follows that for the word 'good' on 'good citizenship' to have an objective meaning, one has to determine what is objectively 'good.' This is a major philosophical question, but without some attempt to address it, the concept of 'good citizenship' remains hopelessly relative, and therefore meaningless. What

[3] Merriam-Webster Dictionary (2025).

[4] Villalobos et al. (2021, p. 14).

[5] Skach (2024, p. 16).

[6] Davies et al. (1999, p. 44).

one must therefore do is define what value system underlies (or should underlie) the value of good citizenship—what one could call the meta value of good citizenship.

1.2 Historical Development of the Concept of Citizenship

The idea of the 'good citizen' has evolved over the centuries in Western thought. This part of the chapter summarises that evolution, focussing on ancient Athenian democracy, Roman republicanism and the development of theories of dignity and human rights from the Renaissance through to the twentieth century.

1.2.1 Athenian Democracy

The starting point for understanding the Ancient Greek concept of citizenship are the writings of Socrates, (469–399 BC), for whom knowledge was the key to acting in accordance with *aretē* or virtue.[7] From this, Socrates concluded that only those who were knowledgeable should govern because only they had the capacity to understand what virtue was and govern in accordance with it.[8]

Socrates' idea was developed by his pupil Plato (c 424–348 BC) who, in his work *Republic* said that the ideal constitution was one which vested authority in the person or people most morally equipped to exercise it, referred to by Plato as 'philosopher-king(s)' (and queens).[9] How the original philosopher kings and queens would be identified and by whom was left vague, but they would perpetuate their class by selective breeding. Their offspring would be trained in philosophy and those who passed the required tests would be next in line to rule. The philosophers would live separately from society, unable to own personal property and, because they were not subject to the temptation to accumulate wealth, would govern solely in the public interest. Plato's preference for rule by philosopher kings led him to reject democracy, on the ground that self-government by the masses would lead to factionalism driven by self-interest.[10]

The works of Aristotle (384–322 BC), who was Plato's pupil, provide the most comprehensive insight into Greek political thought in the fifth century BC. Aristotle's approach differed to that of Plato. In his view, participation in public affairs is not the preserve of the few but is part of human nature, because a human being is inherently a *zoon politikon* (political animal),[11] a being who has the innate ability to live collaboratively in a community called a *polis* where they can achieve their full

[7] Lane (2014, p. 141).

[8] Lane (2014, p. 145).

[9] Lane (2014, pp. 165–6).

[10] Lane (2014, p. 183).

[11] Aristotle *Politics* 1.1253a.

capacity.[12] He described citizens of the *polis* as people who both rule and are ruled,[13] a definition which captures succinctly the complementarity of exercise of power and of subjection to it that defined his view of citizenship. Like Socrates and Plato, he emphasised the central importance that those engaging in politics be guided by *aretē*. However for him, the use of reason to discover what is virtuous, and the achievement of virtuous aims through engagement in politics, were activities that all citizens could and should collaborate in, rather than being the preserve of a select few.[14] Indeed, the exercise of citizenship provided the best conditions for the development of virtue.[15]

However, in contradiction to his apparently universal view of all people being political animals, Aristotle excluded slaves and women as innately lacking an intellect capable of discerning *aretē* and also excluded the poor on the ground that they lacked the leisure time necessary to become educated.[16] Furthermore, although Aristotle considered that government should be shared between those who are 'free and equal'[17] this did not mean that he necessarily considered democracy of the type practised in Athens, in which every citizen, including the poor, had equal power, to be the suitable. Oligarchy in which participation was shared between those distinguished by virtue or some other criterion, such as wealth, could, in his view, also amount to government by equals—that is, equals of this particular class.[18] However, if there was to be a democracy, he proposed that while the broad mass of citizens could participate as equals in choosing office-holders, eligibility to stand for election as an office-holder should be restricted to those meeting a property-ownership requirement, an idea he based on the rather dubious assumption that the wealthy are most likely to have developed an understanding of virtue.[19]

Whatever system of government was adopted, the key for Aristotle was that those engaging in politics be motivated by virtue and a desire to further the common interest rather than for the aggrandisement of personal power or wealth.[20] A system where virtue led citizens to take the interests of all, and not just those of their own class, into account would, he thought, also prevent conflict arising out of social inequality because, for example, in an oligarchy the ruling class would take care not to exploit the poor while in a democracy the masses would not seek to dispossess the wealthy.[21]

Aristotle also took the view that good constitutions and laws were a necessary but not sufficient condition for people to form a political community and for that community to survive. It was also necessary for people to act with friendship (*homonoia*) towards each other. So citizenship not only connected people to the state but also

---

[12] Peterson (2011, p. 35).

[13] Aristotle *Politics* 3.1277b.

[14] Lane (2014, pp. 183–4, 192–3).

[15] Lane (2014, pp. 213–4).

[16] Lane (2014, pp. 185–6).

[17] Aristotle *Politics* 1.255b.

[18] Lane (2014, pp. 200–3).

[19] Lane (2014, pp. 208-10).

[20] Lane (2014, pp. 203–7).

[21] Lane (2014, p. 202).

connected them to each other. As Heater describes the Aristotelian concept of citizenship, 'Citizenship is teamwork; citizenship is shared activity in a spirit of mutual goodwill.'[22] Finally, apart from their right to engage in politics and the ethical obligation to act virtuously, Athenians were expected to act altruistically not only towards family and friends but also towards strangers by engaging in conduct such as nursing the sick, contributing towards those being held for ransom by other states, intervening to protect others from street crime and transporting wounded soldiers.[23]

1.2.2 Civic Republicanism in Rome

The person most responsible for the transfer of Greek political philosophy to Rome was Marcus Tullius Cicero (106–43 BC), who was a lawyer and politician who lived during the tumultuous years that saw the overthrow of the Roman republic. Among the huge volume of his books, letters and speeches is *On Duties* in which he discussed the ideal constitution and what it meant to be a good citizen. The Roman constitution was not a single document but rather comprised a patchwork of laws that had evolved over the centuries in response to class conflict between the patricians and the plebeians, membership of which was defined by birth and wealth.[24] Power was far less broadly distributed than in Athens: If one were to summarise the essential idea underlying the Roman constitution it was that power should be allocated to social groups rather than to individual citizens on an equal basis. In contrast to Athens which, at least in so far as male citizens were concerned, was a genuine democracy, the Roman republic is best described as a managed democracy and, in reality, a de facto oligarchy in which power was concentrated in the hands of a small group of extremely wealthy citizens.

Cicero believed that basing the constitution on the idea of balancing the power of social orders was the key to harmony (*concordia*), which he said would be disrupted if every citizen had equal political power, as that would inevitably lead to the poor seeking redistribution of the property of the rich. This accorded with his view that protection of property rights was the foundation of justice.[25] Therefore, and in contrast to ancient Athens where any citizen could aspire to office, it was only the 'best men'—that is, those of sufficient wealth and social standing—who, Cicero said, should exercise power.[26] Cicero's discussion of what citizenship meant must therefore be understood against a background of what we have seen was a republic based on qualified, rather than full, democracy.

Notwithstanding the narrow allocation of political power in Rome, the values that Cicero said a citizen should live by remain valid in the context of modern democracy.

---

[22] Heater (1999, p. 56).

[23] Sternberg (2006, pp. 174–81).

[24] Lane (2014, pp. 260–7).

[25] Lane (2014, pp. 274–8).

[26] Kennedy (2014, pp. 492–6).

Fundamental to these was the concept of civic republicanism—that citizenship not only conferred rights but also the positive duty to take part in politics. Engagement in public affairs was the epitome of conduct of the good citizen.[27] Citizens' involvement in public affairs was the key to their having control over their own destiny and also provided a defence against tyranny.[28] Of equal importance was the *motive* for involvement in politics which, echoing Aristotle, Cicero said should be for the public good rather than individual ambition.[29] Although ambition was itself a virtue, this was true only in so far it was directed towards justice and towards the benefit of the republic. The duty to act in accordance with the dictates of justice had priority over the interests of the republic and the duties towards both had priority over self-interest, which meant that civic republicanism placed an obligation on the citizen to act in accordance with these duties even if at personal political cost[30]—an injunction which Cicero himself obeyed, and which ultimately led to his assassination as a consequence of his vocal criticism of Marc Anthony's contempt for constitutional government.

Since one could act in the common good only if one understood what it was, Cicero viewed training of young people in philosophy as a precondition for involvement in politics.[31] Far from being elitist, this position reflected egalitarianism, at least within the class excluding slaves and women: Cicero democratised Greek philosophy by writing in Latin, making it accessible to Roman citizens, equipping them for civic engagement. Like Aristotle, Cicero rejected Plato's idea of the best form of government being rule by a philosopher king, because in Cicero's republic, everyone engaged in public affairs should be trained in philosophy.[32] The ability of citizens to participate in politics on an equal basis, and their ownership of, and personal investment in, the republic (a concept which accords with the literal meaning of *res publica* as 'the public thing) provided the best defence against tyranny. By contrast, Cicero considered that if wealth, rather than quality of character came to determine success in politics, the state would degenerate into unequal domination by the few,[33] which is indeed what happened and contributed to the demise of the republic.

Importantly, Cicero stated that all citizens, not only politicians, were subject to duties towards each other.[34] The concept of good citizenship applied to all spheres of life, not just the political, and should guide daily personal interactions. Citizenship was not self-sustaining, nor could it rely solely on legal institutions for its preservation—it had to be lived by people as part of their day-to-day lives in a spirit of community and friendship.[35] The centrality of moral duties to Cicero's concept of

---

[27] Cicero *The Republic* 1.1 and 1.12, *On Duties* 1.72.
[28] Bufacchi (2023, p. 75).
[29] Lane (2014, pp. 281–2).
[30] Bufacchi (2023, p. 41).
[31] Bufacchi (2023, p. 75).
[32] Bufacchi (2023, pp. 75–7).
[33] Cicero *The Republic*, 1.51.
[34] Bufacchi (2023, p. 43).
[35] Heater (1999, p. 55).

civic republicanism which bound members of the community to each other, and its relevance to non-political life, are illustrated by this quote from *On Duties*.[36]

> …we are not born for ourselves alone, but our country claims a share of our being, and our friends a share; and since, as the Stoics hold, everything that the earth produces is created for man's use; and as men, too, are born for the sake of men, that they may be able mutually to help one another; in this direction we ought to follow Nature as our guide, to contribute to the general good by an interchange of acts of kindness, by giving and receiving, and thus by our skill, our industry, and our talents to cement human society more closely together, man to man.

The idea that citizenship imports an obligation to treat others with kindness does not usually occur to us, but it formed an important part of Cicero's view of good citizenship. The implications of this for the modern day are explored later in Chap. 2.

The positive nature of the duties attaching to good citizenship was also evident in Cicero's views on justice. In addressing the fundamental question of how what is good—or just—is to be ascertained, Cicero went no further than saying that what was just was what was in accordance with nature.[37] In this he followed in the steps of Greek natural law philosophers. As we have seen, in the ancient era what was natural was equated with what was ordained by the gods, so both ancient Greek and Roman concepts of goodness and justice were ultimately founded upon religion, even if the content of natural law was ascertained through the application of reason. It was only after the Enlightenment that a concept of justice established on a secular foundation was developed. Nevertheless, Cicero's writings on justice and its opposite—injustice—are still useful.

According to Cicero, injustice consisted of two types: committing unjust acts and failing to shield others from injustice.[38] That failing to prevent injustice—conduct labelled 'passive injustice' by modern theorists[39]—was perceived as injustice itself indicates that the mutuality of obligations that bound citizens to each other might require a person to intervene to assist someone he might not even know. This accords with a principle of Roman law that a person could bring a legal action (the *actio popularis*) on behalf of another or in order to enforce compliance with the constitution, even if their own personal interests had not been harmed.[40] The famously litigious Romans were able to use this to defend the interests of those who might not be able to do so themselves, which constitutes a prime example of positive concern for the wellbeing of another citizen or for the interests of the *res publica* as a whole.

In terms of classic eighteenth and nineteenth century liberal philosophy, the only obligation resting on an individual is negative—the duty not to interfere with the liberty of others.[41] By contrast, Roman republicanism manifested a communitarian strand. While valuing individual liberty and the obligation not to interfere with it,

---

[36] Cicero *On Duties* 1.22.

[37] Cicero *The Laws* 1.17–26.

[38] Cicero *On Duties* 1.23–5.

[39] Schklar (1990, p. 41).

[40] Harris and Harris (2018, pp. 62–5).

[41] Peterson (2011, pp. 11, 14–15).

Roman republicans also believed that individuals had an obligation to ensure the welfare of the community as a whole. This is best exemplified by Cicero's statement 'we are not born for ourselves alone' already quoted, as well as the following which also indicates how Cicero viewed the obligations governing how to treat fellow citizens as being equally binding in relation to foreigners[42]:

> ..we must adhere to the principle that what is useful to the individual is identical to what is useful to the community…as for those who argue that we must take sympathetic account of fellow-citizens but not of outsiders, they are destroying the fellowship common to the human race, and once this is removed, kindness, generosity, goodness and justice are wholly excluded

As Connolly expresses it '…when the Romans talk about politics, they talk about virtue: liberty, patriotism, courage, self-control, securing the common good, self-sacrifice, integrity…'.[43] So the emphasis placed by civic republicanism on citizen interdependence meant that that theory balanced individualism with a civic duty to work in co-operation with other citizens in furtherance of the common good.

Although individual liberty defined as not being subject to the domination of another was an important value of Roman republicanism, the existence of slavery meant that, like the right to political participation, liberty was not shared equally. Furthermore, Roman political philosophy did not recognise anything akin to the modern concept of human rights. Blindness to human rights also meant that Roman communitarianism manifested another obvious flaw when viewed from the modern perspective, which was its failure to take account of economic injustice. Indeed, as already discussed, one of the bases upon which Cicero rejected full democracy was the potential it carried for economic redistribution. It was only in the nineteenth and twentieth centuries that the concept of justice was broadened to include socioeconomic considerations. Nevertheless, Roman thinkers did recognise the importance of preventing arbitrary exercises of power and the need for the legal system to enable individuals to contest such exercises through the courts.[44] As is discussed later in this chapter, placing constraints on arbitrary—in the sense of not rationally justifiable—exercises of power and having available a legal remedy where such exercises occur, are fundamental to the values underlying good citizenship.

Despite this shortcoming, Roman civic republicanism has much to offer the modern world. As is discussed in Chap. 3, there has been a revival of interest in civic republicanism,[45] and it forms the basis of civics education in several countries, most notably in France. The value Roman republicanism attached to the citizen philosopher provides an antidote to modern populism, which relies for its success on voters responding to emotion rather than reason and their being unaccustomed to deliberation and analysis. The central position accorded to philosophy in the education of the citizen would, if emulated now, make the conduct of politics more ethical and, one would hope, mean that the actions of politicians were directed more towards

---

[42] Cicero *On Duties* 3.26–8.

[43] Connolly (2015, p. xv).

[44] Connolly (2015, p. 29).

[45] Peterson (2011, p. 2).

the public interest rather than solely towards the acquisition and retention of power. Even if that overstates the power of education, there is no doubt that inculcating the young with a public ethic would improve the conduct of politics to at least some extent in comparison to its current state. Although different from philosophy, education on civics, another important aspect of the preparation of future citizens, would make citizens more informed and—most importantly—accustomed to informing themselves on public questions, rather than falling prey to the marketing techniques of political parties. The emphasis placed by Roman republicanism on the duty to participate in public affairs means that all citizens provide society with the benefit of their knowledge, which in the modern context would reduce the control over politics that is enjoyed by a relatively small number of people in party hierarchies. Finally, the communitarian nature of Roman republicanism provides a contrary example to the ruthless pursuit of individual interests at the expense of fellow citizens that characterises modern capitalist society.

Cicero provided this bleak depiction of a society where republican virtues are not upheld[46]:

> Everybody demands as much political power as he has force behind him. Reason, moderation, law, tradition, duty count for nothing - likewise the judgement and views of the citizen body and respect for the opinion of those who come after us.

These words could stand as a description of the state of politics in many countries nowadays—democracies included. The next section discusses how developments in political thought during the Renaissance, Enlightenment and the twentieth century expanded the concept of good citizenship, taking as its focus the unifying idea of human dignity.

1.3 Human Dignity as a Fundamental Value

A theme that will often be referred to in this book is the importance of determining what values should underlie society and be reflected in a constitution. Politics and law disjoined from values is a recipe for incoherence, as Wood states '…without philosophy's guidance the state is like a rudderless ship.'[47] As we have seen, Greek and Roman philosophers placed great emphasis on virtue—synonymous with 'goodness'—as the value in accordance with which citizens should conduct themselves. What was 'good' was defined as that which accorded with natural law as ordained by the gods and so was therefore ultimately dependant on faith. This is obviously unsuitable as the foundational value for modern societies which are—or should be—governed by reason. What reason-based value system should guide people in their interactions with each other was addressed by thinkers during the Renaissance and Enlightenment as they escaped the doctrinal strictures imposed by religion.

[46] Cicero *Letters to Brutus* 1.10.

[47] Wood (1991, p. 121).

The starting point used by Renaissance thinkers in addressing this question was the concept of human dignity. In this, they drew upon Cicero, who had said that because of their capacity to reason, which was unique among animals, human beings were entitled to *dignitas*, or dignity.[48] Here it is important to understand that the word *dignitas* had two distinct meanings in ancient Rome. The first was a legal concept and referred to a personal right to bodily integrity, reputation and respect, infringement of which was remediable by means of a civil action for damages called the *actio injuriarum*.[49] The second meaning, referred to by Cicero, was far broader and was a philosophical concept and meant an individual's entitlement to autonomy which imposed on each person a requirement not to interfere with the autonomy of others.[50]

The Renaissance saw a renewed interest in Roman political philosophy, and Cicero's views on dignity were reflected in the writings of the humanist scholar Pico della Mirandola who, in his *Oration on the Dignity of Man*, stated that free will was the essence of man's dignity,[51] from which it followed that interference with free will—autonomy—is an offence against dignity.

The interdependence of dignity and autonomy was developed in the eighteenth century by Immanuel Kant, who stated that 'Autonomy is the ground of the dignity of human nature and of every rational creature,'[52] and that a person should 'Act in such a way that you always treat humanity, whether in your own person or in the person of any other, never as a means but always at the same time as an end.'[53] According to Kant, the inherent dignity of each person made it impermissible for one person to subordinate another or to prevent that other from exercising their free will.[54] Kant also identified equality as a crucial link in the chain linking the 'is' (the fact that the individual has dignity deriving from their autonomy) to the 'ought' (that the individual should be guaranteed rights which prevent interference with that autonomy), arguing that once a person asserts that dignity entitles them to have their autonomy respected, they are logically bound to recognise the same entitlement on the part of all other human beings. So, from the 'is' of one's own dignity proceeds the 'ought' of respecting the dignity of others.[55]

During the second half of the twentieth century, prominent legal philosophers recognised dignity as the fundamental value that should underlie the law.[56] This period saw the development of the McDougal-Laswell school of jurisprudence, the foundation of which was the concept of 'deference for the dignity and worth of the individual.'[57] In developing their school of thought, McDougal and Laswell stated

[48] Cicero *On Duties* 1.105–107.

[49] Justinian *Digest* 47.10.1.2.

[50] Cicero *On Duties* 3.27.

[51] Pico Della Mirandola (1486, p. 6).

[52] Kant (1785, pp. 114–5).

[53] Kant (1785, pp. 106–7).

[54] Kant (1785, pp. 161–2).

[55] Feinberg (1986, pp. 27–51).

[56] Fuller (1964, p. 162), Raz (1979) and Waldron (2012).

[57] Lasswell and McDougal (1943, p. 207).

that the 'supreme value of democracy is the dignity and worth of the individual; hence a democratic society is a commonwealth of mutual deference.'[58] They emphasised the universality of the entitlement to dignity by describing it as 'the primary postulate of public order, infusing and transcending all particular communities,'[59] arguing that dignity was the ultimate value which human rights were to serve.[60] In keeping with this McDougal, Lasswell and Chen identified specific rights that needed to be guaranteed in order for human dignity to be respected.[61]

In the twentieth century the concept of human dignity formed what Neal refers to as the 'substantive basic norm'[62] underlying the human rights documents which were adopted by the United Nations in the wake of the human rights abuses that occurred during World War II. The Preamble to the Universal Declaration of Human Rights states 'the inherent dignity and the equal and inalienable rights of all members of the human family is the foundation of freedom, justice and peace in the world', while Article 1 of the Declaration states that 'All human beings are born free and equal in dignity and rights.' Both these provisions clearly owe much to the Kantian view of the inherent dignity of human beings, the equal freedom that that dignity implies, and of the consequent entitlement of each human individual to fundamental rights. Dignity is also protected by Article 10 of the *International Covenant on Civil and Political Rights*,[63] and Article 13 of the *International Covenant on Economic, Social and Cultural Rights*.[64]

Dignity is also referred to in the constitutions of various jurisdictions. In Germany and South Africa dignity is not only protected as a specific right but is also the touchstone in accordance with which the constitution as a whole is interpreted.[65] In Germany, Article 1(1) of the constitution states that 'Human dignity shall be inviolable. To respect and protect it shall be the duty of all state authority.'[66] Article 1(2) states that 'The German people therefore acknowledge inviolable and inalienable human rights as the basis of every community, of peace and of justice in the world'. The use of the word 'therefore' is important, because it shows that, in the mind of the drafters, dignity could not be upheld unless fundamental rights were protected as the tangible manifestations of dignity.[67] In South Africa the constitution states 'The Republic of South Africa is one, sovereign, democratic state founded on the following values: (a) Human dignity, the achievement of equality and the advancement of

58 Lasswell and McDougal (1943, p. 212).

59 Lasswell and McDougal (1971, p. 393).

60 Shestack (1984, p. 96).

61 McDougal et al. (1980).

62 Neal (2014, pp. 37–8).

63 GA Res 2200A (XXI) of 16 December 1966.

64 GA RES 2200A (XXI) of 16 December 1966.

65 In Germany see the *Lüth Case* 7 BVerfGE 198, 205 (1958) and in South Africa *Carmichele v Minister of Safety and Security* 2001 (4) SA 938 (CC).

66 *Basic Law of the Federal Republic of Germany 1949*. For an overview of the foundational role of dignity in the German constitution see Grote (2014), pp. 196–207).

67 Eberle (2012, p. 206).

human rights and freedoms.'[68] Chapter 2 of the constitution protects a wide range of political, social and economic rights, with dignity included as a free-standing right in s 10, which states that 'Everyone has inherent dignity and the right to have their dignity respected and protected'. In India, the preamble to the constitution refers to the promotion of dignity is one of the purposes underlying the constitution[69] and dignity has been used as the foundation for the interpretation of the fundamental rights provisions on the constitution.[70]

1.4 Rawls' Theory and Human Dignity

As discussed in the previous section, the origin of the idea that human dignity is the supreme value lies in Cicero's argument that the capacity of human beings to reason and thus to make decisions through the application of free will means that each person is autonomous and that that autonomy is deserving of respect. But that does not answer the question of *why* society should be based on respect for the equal autonomy of each person. Why should society not be based on the principle that those who are capable of securing power should not use it to dominate others? This was the theory advanced by Friedrich Nietzsche, who argued that it is more efficient, and more conducive to the survival of humankind if society is not based upon moral principles but rather on the idea that those who are endowed with strength and ability should dominate the rest of humankind[71] unconstrained by external ethical rules[72]—which in essence means a society whose underlying principle is survival of the fittest.

An answer to this was provided by the legal philosopher, John Rawls. Rawls addressed the question of whether it was possible to provide a rational justification for universal values. He posited a method for answering this question which involved a hypothetical exercise in which a random group of people were asked to agree on a set of fundamental rules for a society that they would then live in.[73] However, while doing this, they would operate under the important constraint that they would be behind what Rawls called a 'veil of ignorance'.[74] This meant that they would not know what either their identity or circumstances would be in the new society—their gender, ethnicity, socio-economic class, religion, physical capacity or history of prior conduct—until after they had devised the fundamental rules.

Rawls said that in a situation where 'no one knows his place in society, his class position or social status; nor does he know his fortune in the distribution of natural

[68] *Republic of South Africa Constitution Act 1996.*

[69] *Constitution of India 1949.*

[70] Baruah (2022, pp. 25–31).

[71] Nietzche (1895, p. 104).

[72] Nietzche (1886, pp. 113–4).

[73] Rawls (1972, pp. 17–22).

[74] Rawls (1972, pp. 136–42).

assets and abilities, his intelligence and strength, and the like',[75] rational participants would agree on what he called the 'liberty principle', namely that each person should have the fullest degree of liberty as is consistent with everyone-else's equal liberty[76] and the 'equality principle,' that social and economic opportunities should be arranged so as to be of greatest benefit to the least advantaged and also in such a way that there is substantive, and not merely theoretical, equality of opportunity.[77] In reaching this dual imperative to protect individual liberty as well as the welfare of society, Rawls' principles are consistent with civic republicanism which, it will be recalled, valued both individualism and communitarianism. However, Rawls takes the obligations imposed by communitarianism a step further than those recognised in ancient Rome by requiring protection from socio-economic justice.

When applied to constitutional design, Rawls' liberty principle requires that the legislative and executive power of the state be limited by protection of civil liberties, and the equality principle by protection of socio-economic rights by means of a justiciable bill of rights.[78] In tandem they protect individuals from deprivation of their rights by majorities and provide a minimum level of material security. As Heater states[79]

> There should be....some balance... between freedom and rights for the individual on the one hand and commitment and duties to the community on the other. Without such a balance, civic virtue is submerged by selfishness. A society of selfish individuals is, at its extreme, no society at all, nor does it have citizens, properly speaking – it is nothing more than an agglomeration of competitive units. And self-seeking competitiveness generates stresses and resentments that are the very antithesis of the republican vision of a harmonious, co-operative, community, in which self-interest and the interest of the community are in some sense identical.

The strength of Rawls' theory is its appeal both to individualism (in that it protects freedom) and to altruism (in that it protects against disadvantage). The device of the veil of ignorance ensures that empathy plays a role in rule-making because it forces people to consider how they would feel if their identity or circumstances were completely different from what they currently are, answering difficult questions such as 'How would I want to be treated if I was a prisoner?' It embodies what late nineteenth century French Prime Minister Léon Bourgeois referred to as the doctrine of 'solidarism,' which held that society as a whole should work together, with the rich helping the poor, its motto being 'Every man is his neighbour's debtor.'[80] It also echoes the Marxist view that 'emancipation' means more than the absence of control over individual liberty, and that true emancipation is possible only in an equal society in which 'the condition for the free development of each is the condition for

[75] Rawls (1972, p. 137).

[76] Rawls (1972, p. 60).

[77] Rawls (1972, pp. 60, 303).

[78] Rawls (1982, p. 6, 1999, p. 80).

[79] Heater (1999, p. 72).

[80] Fenby (2015, p. 217).

the free development of all.'[81] What Rawls' theory shows is that, if stripped of prejudices arising from identity and circumstance, rational people will choose to limit the power of the state so as to preserve a zone of personal autonomy for him or herself but will also set a minimum standard of socio-economic equality. Although Rawls was not directly concerned with the concept of dignity, his theory provides a rational justification for human dignity as a fundamental value that must underlie an objectively good society. These rules reflect the individualistic and communitarian aspects of good citizenship and the need for the good citizen to balance self-interest with the broader social interest when engaging in public affairs.

Recognition of human dignity as the fundamental social value has the effect of broadening what is meant by 'good citizenship.' Theorists speaking from their own particular ideological positions suggest that there are different types of good citizenship. Pykett et al. observe that[82]

> Republicans see good citizens as ideally possessing certain virtues and oriented primarily to the collective good of the community. Liberals see good citizens as individuals, with rights and freedoms, who respect the rights and freedoms of others as they pursue their interests. Socialists see good citizens as seekers and defenders of social and economic equality. Greens see good citizens as those who live sustainably, and encourage the same in social and political institutions.

Yet I would argue that all of these values are inherent in good citizenship because each of them relates to an interest which must be defended in order to ensure human dignity.

This part of the chapter began by examining the concept of citizenship as understood in ancient Athens and Rome. The fact that only a narrow class of people enjoyed political rights in those societies, and that the moral values underlying citizenship did not extend to concepts such as human rights and socio-economic equality, meant that citizenship as conceived of in the classical world was not based on the concept of dignity as it is now understood. Yet Cicero's recognition that human beings were entitled to dignity by virtue of their capacity to reason constituted the first step in the development of dignitarian theory. And notwithstanding the absence of concepts such as universal and equal entitlement to rights, including rights to socio-economic justice, from his conception of what constitutes good citizenship, the emphasis he placed on citizen knowledge of philosophy, the duty to participate in public affairs, the communitarian value of acting in the public interest rather than only for personal advantage, and the virtue of kindness are values that are relevant to citizenship today.

---

[81] Fulbrook (2005, p. 143).

[82] Pykett et al. (2010, p. 524).

References

Aristotle. Politics. Rackham H (trans) (1944) Aristotle in 23 volumes. London, William Heinemann Ltd.

Baruah P (2022) Human dignity in Indian constitutional adjudication. In: Hsu J (ed) Human dignity in Asia – dialogue between law and culture. Cambridge University Press, Cambridge, pp 21–39

Bufacchi V (2023) Why Cicero matters. Bloomsbury, London

Cicero *Letters to Brutus*. D Shackleton Bailey (trans) J Henderson (ed) (2002) Harvard University Press, Cambridge.

Cicero. The Republic. Rudd N (trans) (1998a) The republic and the laws. Oxford University Press, Oxford.

Cicero. The Laws. Rudd N (trans) (1998b) The republic and the laws. Oxford University Press, Oxford.

Cicero. On Duties. Miller W (trans) (1913) De Officiis. Harvard University Press, Cambridge.

Connolly J (2015) The life of roman republicanism. Princeton University Press, Princeton

Davies I, Gregory I, Riley S (1999) Good citizenship and educational provision. Taylor & Francis, London

Eberle E (2012) Observations on the development of human dignity and personality in German constitutional law: an overview. Liverpool Law Rev 33:201–33

Feinberg J (1986) Harm to self. Oxford University Press, Oxford

Fenby J (2015) The history of modern France from the revolution to the war on terror. Simon & Schuster, London

Fulbrook M (2005) The people's state – East German society from Hitler to Honecker. Yale University Press, New Haven

Fuller L (1964) The Morality of Law. Yale University Press, New Haven.

Grote R (2014) The German Rechtsstaat in a comparative perspective. In: Silkenat J, Hickey J, Barenboim P (eds) The legal doctrines of the rule of law and the legal state (Rechtsstaat). Cham, Spinger

Harris B, Harris E (2018) Interfering busybody or public-minded citizen? The actio popularis as a model for reform of the rules of standing in constitutional cases in Australia. J Politics Law 11:62–78

Heater D (1999) What is citizenship? Polity Press, Cambridge

Humanity International (2009) The role of éducation civique in the creation of French citoyens. Humanity International, Brooklyn

Justinina. Digest. Mommsen T, Kreuger P, Watson A (trans) (1985) The digest of Justinian. University of Pennsylvania, Philadelphia

Kant I (1785) Groundwork of the metaphysic of morals. Paton H (trans) (2005). Taylor & Francis, London

Kennedy G (2014) Cicero, roman republicanism and the contested meaning of *Libertas*. Political Stud 62:488–501

Lane M (2014) Greek and Roman political ideas. Penguin, London

Lasswell H, McDougal M (1943) Legal education and public policy: professional training in the public interest. Yale Law J 52(1943):203–295

Lasswell H, McDougal M (1971) Criteria for a theory about law. Southern Calif Law Rev 44(1971):362–395

McDougal M, Laswell H, Chen L (1980) Human rights and world public order. Yale University Press, New Haven

Merriam-Webster Dictionary (2025) Merriam-Webster, Springfield

Neal M (2014) Respect for human dignity as substantive basic norm. Int J Law Context 10:26–46

Nietzche F (1886) Zimmern H (trans) (2010) Beyond good and evil: prelude to a philosophy of the future. SoHo Books, Lexington

Nietzsche F (1895) Wayne T (trans) (2004) Ecce homo – how one becomes what one is & the antichrist – a curse on Christianity. Algora Publishing, New York

Peterson A (2011) Civic republicanism and civic education: the education of citizen. Palgrave Macmillan UK, Houndmills

Pico Della Mirandola G (1486) Oration on the dignity of man. Caponigri A (trans) (1956) Gateway, South Bend

Pykett J, Saward M, Schaefer A (2010) Framing the good citizen. Br J Politics Int Relat 12:523–38

Rawls J (1972) A theory of justice. Clarendon Press, Oxford

Rawls J (1999) The law of peoples: with "The Idea of Public Reason Revisited." Harvard University Press, Cambridge

Rawls J (1982) The basic liberties and their priority. In: McMurrin S (ed) The Tanner lectures on human values. University of Utah Press, Salt Lake City.

Raz J (1979) The rule of law and its virtue. In: Raz J (ed) The authority of law: essays on law and morality. Oxford University Press, Oxford

Schklar J (1990) The faces of injustice. Yale University Press, New Haven

Shestack J (1984) The jurisprudence of human rights in Theodore Meron (ed) Human rights in international law (Clarendon Press, Oxford), p 69

Skach C (2024) How to be a citizen - learning to rely less on riles and more on each other. Bloomsbury Publishing, London

Sternberg R (2006) Tragedy offstage: suffering and sympathy in ancient Athens. University of Texas Press, Austin

Villalobos C, Morel M, Trevino E (2021) What is a "Good Citizen"? A systematic literature review. In: Trevino E, Carrasco D, Claes E, Kennedy K (eds) Good citizenship for the next generation – a global perspective using IEA ICCS 2016 data. Springer International, Cham

Waldron J (2012) How law protects dignity. Cambridge Law J 71:200–222

Wood N (1991) Cicero's social and political thought. University of California Press, Berkeley

Chapter 2
The Practice of Good Citizenship

Abstract If respect for human dignity forms the basis of good citizenship, what practises should a person cultivate in order to be a good citizen? This chapter proposes that there are four key practices—reason, tolerance, civic participation and kindness—which are necessary for good citizenship to flourish: reason, tolerance, participation and kindness. Decision-making by the use of reason—and rejection of its opposite, which is arbitrariness—lies at the heart of a society based on human dignity. Yet, even in democracies, reason faces challenges from religious-based decision-making which substitutes subjective belief for objective deliberation, conservatism which sees inquiry into progress as futile and populism which substitutes decision-making based on emotion for that based on analysis. Reason-based decision-making is directed towards the ascertainment of the truth, which in turn depends on tolerance of adverse opinion, because consideration of the widest possible range of views maximises the likelihood of truth being discovered. Participation in public life, and in particular participation in political processes, is the way in which people give effect to the values underlying good citizenship and contribute to the common good. The level of public participation in a society is therefore a barometer of its citizens' commitment to it. Finally, the willingness of people to engage in public participation is affected by the way in which others interact with them, hence the importance of kindness, civility and altruism, which help build social capital.

2.1 The Practice of Good Citizenship

Chapter 1 discussed the theory that underpins good citizenship, concluding that good citizenship requires respect for human dignity. But how is the theory of good citizenship to be manifested in practice? As Peterson states, referring specifically to civic republicanism[1]

> ...civic republicanism embodies an active conception of what it means to be a citizen, with citizenship defined *as a practice*. To be a citizen is to act in a particular way and within a particular political community.

[1] Peterson (2011, p. 3).

B. Harris, *Cultivating Good Citizenship*,
SpringerBriefs in Law, https://doi.org/10.1007/978-981-92-2740-2_2

He further states that civic involvement 'requires citizens to develop and possess certain attributes and dispositions—that is, civic virtue.'[2] What practices should a person adopt in order to demonstrate civic virtue, thereby becoming a good citizen? This chapter posits four of these—reason, tolerance, participation and kindness.

2.2 Reason and the Challenges It Faces

The capacity to use reason lies at the heart of Rawls' methodology for the identification of objective values and is self-evidently a cornerstone of good citizenship. This section discusses the importance of reason-based decision-making. It also examines the threat posed to it by religion, conservatism and populism. Authoritarian regimes, where government is based on overtly arbitrary decision-making, obviously pose a greater danger to reason-based decision-making than do these phenomena. However, the reason for focussing on them is that they pose a more subtle threat to freedom because those who base decision-making on these concepts do so within the framework of free and democratic systems.

2.2.1 The Importance of Reason

Reason-based decision making is fundamental to the operation of a just society. Its antithesis is arbitrary government. Arbitrariness may, in the worst instances, manifest itself as true senselessness, where decisions are irrational, erratic and based on the whim of the ruler. More commonly, however, arbitrary government takes the form of decision-making which is not senseless but is designed to further the objectives of the government while rejecting the obligation to provide a rational justification for them. This type of arbitrariness is enabled by structural flaws in the constitutional system, in particular the unavailability either of judicial review of administrative action or of a bill of rights against which the courts can test the validity of legislation and executive action. To take a simple example, assume that a law granted wide discretion to a government department to grant driver's licences, and the department instituted a policy that licences would not be granted to people with brown hair. Such a policy and the decisions made under it would fit the legal definition of arbitrariness, because having brown hair is not a consideration that is rationally connected to the capacity to drive.

When applied to the field of government, reason-based decision-making supports the principle that the exercise of power by one person over another is justifiable only

[2] Peterson (2011, p. 77).

if demonstrably reasonable.[3] This is referred to as the doctrine of public justifiability.[4] Arbitrariness is obviously incompatible with public justifiability. From the perspective of process, public justifiability requires decision makers to respect the arguments of others and be prepared to defend their own position on rational grounds. In a system where the need for public justifiability is respected, it is insufficient that the state has the power to make a decision—the decision must be one that is supported by rational argument, and the rights of citizens are protected by their ability to contest exercises of power by the state.[5]

Deliberation is the process that gives practical effect to public justifiability. It requires the use of reasoned argument to justify one's position and, crucially, obliges one to give due consideration to the arguments of others. Habituation to explanation of one's own views and taking into account the views of others has a positive effect on politics in that it increases the likelihood of decisions being reached through consensus but, even when consensus is not reached, at least leads the 'losers' of a political argument to acknowledge that they were respected as members of the body politic and their views were heard.[6]

What do we mean by decisions which are based on reason and are therefore reasonable? Much depends on the ethical framework under which rationality is assessed—for example, a tyrannical regime could comply with the standard of reasonable justification by demonstrating that a decision was necessary for it to maintain domination over the population. It follows from the discussion in Chap. 1 of what 'good' citizenship means, that the term 'rational' must be given the qualified meaning of what is rational in accordance with human dignity and the principles of justice that it implies. It may be that such a qualification is otiose given the argument that Rawls' reason-based model of determining rules for society leads to his principles of justice—in other words that reason, in the realm of values determination inevitably leads to justice. Nevertheless, it is useful to remind ourselves that when we speak of rationality, we mean what is rational within a framework built on justice.

When applied to law, and human rights law in particular, reason-based law making requires that a limitation of a right of a person is justifiable only if the limitation is directed towards the achievement of a justifiable objective, that the limitation goes no further than is necessary to achieve the objective and that there is proportionality between the extent to which the right is limited and the importance of the objective. This test, usually referred to as the 'proportionality test' has been adopted, with minor differences in formulation, in various jurisdictions.[7]

---

[3] Mason (2007, p. 679).

[4] Wall (2016, pp. 204–5).

[5] Peterson (2011, pp. 103–4).

[6] Peterson (2011, pp. 109–11).

[7] See for example the decision of the Supreme Court of Canada in *R v Oakes* [1986] 1 S.C.R. 103, 138–40, the formulation contained in s 36 of the *Constitution of the Republic of South Africa* and by the High Court of Australia in *McCloy v New South Wales* (2015) 257 CLR 178, 194–5.

It is no hyperbole to say that we live in an age where the gains of the Enlightenment are under threat by denial of objective facts[8] and as emotion and religious faith threaten to replace reason as the basis for policy making. That emotion can be used as a political tool of persuasion has long been recognised. In *On Rhetoric,* Aristotle noted that an audience may be persuaded as much by emotion (*pathos*) as by reason (*logos*).[9] Political figures have become increasingly accustomed to appeal to fear, because of the powerful response it elicits—as President Macron stated in an interview in 2022 'Argumentation is less powerful than emotion, and negative emotion is more powerful than positive emotion.'[10] This phenomenon has manifested itself in numerous countries, particularly in the context of immigration policy where migrants, as outsiders, are cast as a threat to society and are subjected to unfounded accusations of criminality, a phenomenon which is common in the United States,[11] the United Kingdom[12] and Australia.[13]

Fomentation of hatred aside, unreason has been deployed as a strategy to avoid decisions which are costly, inconvenient or against political interest, often taking the form of attacks on science, including by denigration of individual scientists—or indeed scientists as an entire class—as members of a nefarious, power-hungry 'elite'.[14] The most obvious example of this is denial of anthropogenic climate change.[15] Another is denial that COVID19 was a distinct disease or that mask-wearing and vaccination are necessary and effective to prevent its spread.[16] Such claims rely on a rejection of objective observation, analysis and experimentation required by scientific method. There is irony in the fact that while the assault on science nowadays emanates predominantly from the right,[17] it has its roots in the rejection of objective truth by postmodernists of the left in the second half of the twentieth century.[18] Their rejection of reason was based on the writings of French linguists who said that since each word has meaning only in relation to other words, no word has meaning.[19] If words have no objective meaning it follows that it is impossible to say anything is true, and since there is no truth there are no facts—rather everyone has their own 'story' which is equally valid as any other. It is upon

---

[8] Shapiro (2024, p. 3).

[9] Aristotle *On Rhetoric* 1.2.

[10] CBS News (2022). The phenomenon whereby negative ideas are more likely to be retained than positive ones is known as negativity bias in psychology and is the product of the survival imperative instinct which predisposes the mind to focus attention on that which is threatening—see Rozin and Royzman (2001).

[11] BBC News (2024a), Villareal (2024), Sullivan (2024).

[12] Morris (2013), Syal (2023).

[13] Anderson (2016), Karp (2018), Reilly (2019).

[14] Nogrady (2024).

[15] Washington (2011, pp. 43–63, 95–7).

[16] Golec de Zavala (2024, pp. 148–54).

[17] Oreskes and Conway (2022).

[18] Kuntz (2012).

[19] Sarup (1993, pp. 32–4).

this foundation that the current 'post-truth' political culture, in which facts are of no importance, is based.

2.2.2 *Religious-Based Decision-Making*

Reason-based decision-making has also faced increasing challenge by religion. Tolerance for believers (and non-believers), and a recognition that there should be no established religion, were key achievements of the Enlightenment, yet in some countries this principle has never been accepted while in others it is subject to attack. The importance of these Enlightenment principles are obvious but bear repeating: Basing policy on the tenets of a particular religion infringes the right to religious freedom because people are mandated to live in accordance with a belief system of which they are not adherents. It is also inconsistent with the right to equality, because the adoption of a particular religion by the state obviously involves discrimination against all others, it being noteworthy that proponents of religious-based policy are obviously unable to explain—other than by reference to faith—why their particular religion is the 'true' religion. This brings one to the heart of the problem: Where religious doctrine forms the ultimate authority for state policy, 'debate' on public questions in the true sense of the word is foreclosed because ultimately the answers to such questions are determined not in accordance with observation and analysis and the evaluation of competing views, but rather in accordance with subjective beliefs, usually contained in a religious text which, it is stated, contains the will of a deity as revealed to a prophet. What 'is', in the sense of which is true, is therefore determined in accordance with the divine will, to which adherents permit neither doubt not contradiction.

The degree to which religion forms the basis of state policy in different countries ranges across a spectrum, from theocracies such as Afghanistan and Iran where there is no distinction between religious doctrine and law and where ultimate power is held by clerics, to Pakistan which is proclaimed as being an Islamic state but which is governed by secular institutions, to Indonesia where there is no official religion but where everyone must declare that they belong to one of the six officially recognised religions, and to the United Kingdom where the Church of England of which the monarch is head is the official religion but where religious doctrine has no effect on public policy.

In the United States the influence of religion has most notably been manifested in a rejection of secularism by elements of the political right and the rise of Christian nationalism, an ideology which states that public power should be founded upon, and be directed towards the implementation of, Christian values.[20] Despite the fact that separation of church and state and religious freedom are constitutionally protected by the First Amendment, moves such as the removal of books considered incompatible

[20] Goldberg (2006, pp. 5–8).

with Christian values from school libraries, ostensibly in order to protect minors,[21] and the teaching of the Bible, ostensibly as history,[22] threaten to achieve de facto what would be impermissible if presented as an overt establishment of religion. Such policies may ultimately be struck down on First Amendment grounds in accordance with the doctrine that whether a measure infringes a constitutional right is tested with reference not only to what it provides on its face but also 'as applied' that is, in light of its practical effect in particular circumstances.[23] However these examples are indicative of a conflict over the fundamental question of whether public policy should be determined subjectively in accordance with faith or objectively in accordance with reason.

The impact of religion on public policy is further illustrated by the fact that in both the United States[24] and Australia[25] politicians have claimed a divine mandate to run for office. Of course, in a society where the rights to freedom of opinion, religion and expression are protected, a person is free to stand for office whatever their motivation and to justify their political views by referring to religious beliefs if they choose, but a more disturbing phenomenon is where, once in office, leaders claim that their policy decisions are divinely directed—an example being the statement by George W Bush that God told him to invade Iraq.[26] This is incompatible with the principle of public justification that underlies a reason-based order: A person claiming to do divinely-ordained work is driven by faith and so, once set upon a course of action, is by definition not amenable to dissuasion through reason-based argument. Indeed, in instances where a leader believes that a course of action has been divinely mandated, departure from it would involve disobedience to God, which a person of faith could obviously not contemplate.[27] The intermingling of religious faith and political power raises the prospect of arbitrary government based on the precepts of unprovable dogma. The law does provide recourse in the form of administrative law review (or constitutional review, but only where a country's constitution contains a bill of rights) in cases where executive decisions are not reasonably justifiable. The point, however, is that in a society where reason-based decision-making is respected as an element of good citizenship, such challenges would not be necessary.

As a contrast to this, one can point to the example of France, where the concept of *laïcité*, or secularism, is established in Article 1 of the constitution, which defines France as a secular republic. To that extent, France is similar to the United States, but secularism goes further than in the United States because the concept is not only protected by law but is deeply embedded as a value in French society. So while private

[21] Marcos (2024). The same has occurred in Australia, see Cassidy and Rose (2024).

[22] Salam and Pengelly (2024).

[23] *United States v Salerno* 481 U.S. 739 (1987) 745, *Sabri v. United States* 541 U.S. 600 (2004) 604.

[24] Tiwari (2024).

[25] Martin (2021), Hardaker (2021).

[26] MacAskill (2005).

[27] Morrison (2024, p. 30), Shepherd (2024).

religious belief is protected, public affairs are kept free from the influence of religion,[28] leading France to be described as a country where there is both freedom of religion and freedom from religion.[29] As a consequence, politicians refrain from introducing religious principles into public debate and usually do not disclose whether they have any religious belief. The embedding of secularism into French culture has the effect of making secularism far stronger than in the United States, and acts as a prophylactic against the formation of policy other than on rational grounds.

This is not to deny the right of religious bodies, in common with other social groups, to make representations on public policy. History provides examples of church criticism of state policy having salutary effect. To cite two diverse examples, churches in South Africa took a prominent role in resisting apartheid,[30] while in the DDR, churches provided an umbrella under which protesters could take refuge, to the extent that the events of 1989 leading to the fall of the Berlin wall and the establishment of democratic institutions have been referred to as the 'Protestant revolution.'[31] It is also interesting to note that the positions taken by religious bodies, even if dictated by religious doctrine, may sometimes accord with those indicated by the secular value of human dignity. This is unsurprising—the Rawlsian device of determining values by imagining ones-self in the shoes of others accords with the tenet common to many faiths that one should treat others as one would want to be treated ones-self.[32] However, the circumstance where a government receives representations from religious bodies and then subjects them to rational analysis is very different from that where religious dogma forms the basis of government policy. How can any particular religion form the basis of state policy given that in every society there are adherents of different religions and adherents of none?

There is no doubt that many countries face a clash of values over the character of society, between those advocating faith-based policy-making on the one hand and those seeking to uphold the principle of secular policy-making on the other. That this is appreciated by the former camp is clear, as demonstrated by the statement by former Australian Prime Minister, Scott Morrison that 'We should continue to be bold in the confession of our faith and not be intimidated by the secularization of our society that will increasingly oppress Christians',[33] an assertion which is both revealing in its admission of the existence of a culture war and disingenuous in its depiction of secularisation as oppression, a position that is comprehensible only from the stance of a world view that Christians have a right to mould society according to their beliefs, and that basing the institutions of the state on religious neutrality amounts to a denial of that right. The assault on reason threatens to create an environment in which decisions relating to the application of state power are arbitrary, unpredictable and not justifiable on the basis of reason, which underscores how crucial is the principle

[28] The Economist (2020).

[29] Donadio (2021, p. 72).

[30] Wallis and Holliday (1989).

[31] Fulbrook (2008, pp. 208, 265).

[32] Scott and Seglow (2007, pp. 6–7).

[33] Morrison (2024, p. 77).

of reason to the idea of good citizenship—to use a classical metaphor, there is no place for religion in the forum.

2.2.3 *Conservatism*

The origins of modern conservatism are traced to the eighteenth century Anglo-Irish politician and political philosopher Edmund Burke who, in his *Reflections on the revolution in France*,[34] expressed horror at the violence that occurred in France that followed the overthrow of the Bourbon monarchy, which Burke saw as the consequence of a vain attempt to create a new society based on abstract principles developed during the Enlightenment.[35] It is on his observations that the fundamental principle of conservatism is based—that people are not perfectible and that social stability depends on the maintenance of the power of institutions in which it was traditionally located which, in the eighteenth century were the monarchy, aristocracy, army, church and family. Arguably, however, the lesson of the French revolution is that conservativism is a failure even on its own terms in that its objective of prioritising stability and resisting change is unlikely to work in circumstances where resentment against injustice builds to the extent that it leads to revolution. These institutions were considered the 'natural' repositories of power not because their power-holding was justified on the basis of any theory but because they had successfully secured and maintained power as a matter of historical fact. Progressives' attempts at reform directed towards changing this 'natural' order by placing power in the hands of the masses were considered by conservatives to be a recipe for chaos.[36] It is in light of this that the term used by conservative parties in the United Kingdom and in Australia that they are the 'natural party of government'—which is senseless on the face of it—can be understood, in that it reflects the idea that the party which seeks to maintain the natural order is the party that deserves to be in power.

The anti-theoretical nature of conservatism means that it rejects the idea that analysis of the human condition can provide a roadmap towards the establishment of an ideal society. Yet it is puzzling why conservatives who (presumably) accept the fact that progress is possible in medicine, engineering, psychology and every other area of human endeavour should insist that it is not possible in relation to the development of social conditions. When applied to constitution-making, conservatives reject the idea of framing a constitution in accordance with abstract universal principles applicable to humankind, and instead argue that the most suitable constitution emerges organically as a consequence of historical events and the development of tradition.[37] In its belief in the maintenance of power structures which arise naturally, conservatism has much in common with the Nietzschean idea that society operates best on the basis of

[34] Burke (1790).

[35] Nisbet (2002, pp. 19–20).

[36] Nisbet (2002, pp. 50–3).

[37] Nisbet (2002, pp. 42–3).

the survival of the fittest and that curbing power in pursuit of an ethical value such as justice causes a society to become effete. Both Nietzschean and conservative theory justify the accrual of power to those whose natural abilities have enabled them to acquire it.

Despite its name, it is incorrect to define conservatism as 'preservation' and to characterise conservatives as inherently opposed to change. Opposition to change holds true only in circumstances where a conservative order is in place and requires defence against progressives seeking to overturn it. In cases where power structures do not align with the conservative vision, conservatives will engage in radical change to (re)establish the traditional order. As examples of this one can cite the economic and social policies implemented by Conservative governments in the United Kingdom and neo-conservative elements of the Republican party in the United States since the 1980s. It would however be mistake to think that conservatism is a feature only of parties on the right of the political spectrum.[38] It is also possible to conceive of left-wing conservatives, as in the example from the mid-1970s when, during the struggle for power that occurred in the wake of Mao's death, commentators referred to 'conservative' elements in the Chinese Communist Party who were fighting to protect the political and economic order that Mao had established. Thus, what position conservatives adopt depends entirely on what is considered to be the 'natural order' that must be defended, an order that can be based on a variety of ideologies.

Conservativism displays an ambiguous attitude towards human rights. Consistent with the view that natural power relationships should not be disturbed, Burkean conservatives vehemently opposed the idea that governmental power should be subject to restraint by a bill of rights. This is despite the fact that in the eighteenth century, human rights were referred to as 'natural rights.' The explanation for this apparent paradox lies in the difference between what Enlightenment thinkers meant by the word 'natural' (that which is indicated by the application of reason) and the meaning ascribed to the word by conservatives (that which occurs naturally). So to conservatives, what is of the greatest importance is the preservation of what they consider to be the natural order. Whether that order is just or is consistent with human rights theory is unimportant. Consistent with this mindset, conservatives opposed the extension of the franchise in nineteenth century Britain because it would lead to a shift in the balance of electoral power to a social class whose members had not historically exercised it because they did not own sufficient property. They also resisted the granting of the franchise to women in the early twentieth century and subsequent legislative measures designed to ensure women's equality because they saw these as likely to lead to women moving out of their 'natural' roles as wives and mothers.[39] The same applied to measures designed to ameliorate the effect of discrimination against other groups. The ethical basis of institutional power is not of

[38] The designations 'right' and 'left' originate in the seating arrangements in the National Assembly during the French revolutionary era, when supporters of the monarchy sat on the right of the speaker and their opponents on the left.

[39] Nisbet (2002, p. 63).

interest to conservatives. The ideology is, at its core, pragmatic, and justifies itself on the basis of outcomes—social stability above all—rather than by reference to abstract principle. To conservatives it is more important that society is stable rather than just.

The pragmatism—and indeed amorality—that lies at the heart of conservatism is perhaps no better illustrated than by late 18th and early nineteenth century conservatives' attitudes to slavery in the British empire. Conservatives doggedly opposed both efforts to end the slave trade and the emancipation of slaves, arguing that the latter would destroy the economic viability of planters' businesses in the Caribbean.[40] This argument was entirely correct from a pragmatic point of view, but obviously inconsistent with human dignity. The point, however, was that to conservatives there was no 'right' both to be a slave (at least in the case of people not in Britain, where it was prohibited by the common law). In their view, whether slavery was lawful or not depended on the views of society at the time.

Despite their rejection of human rights ideology, conservatives express a degree of support for liberties such as freedom of speech, freedom of religion and the right to due process. Despite this, conservatives defend legislative supremacy and have opposed the idea of introducing bills of rights in countries such as Australia on the ground that the power of the state should not be subject to control by the courts.[41] In any event it is clear that, conservatives' commitment to civil liberties is decidedly conditional and will be trumped by what they see as the higher value of preserving order, as witness the large-scale deprivation of civil liberties that occurred in countries, including the United States, the United Kingdom and Australia, following the 9/11 attack, where legislation which curtailed civil liberties was enacted as part of the so-called 'war on terror.'[42]

One area in which conservatives are committed to liberty is that pertaining to the rights to property and to engage in economic activity.[43] Burke had seen protection of property as a key aspect of conservatism, but it was the late twentieth century that saw conservatives adopt the language of individual freedom in support of policies such as reduction in taxation, the weakening of workers' rights and de-regulation of equity financial markets in an effort to maximise opportunities for wealth creation. The effect of this was to broaden opportunities for the wealthy to exploit what conservatives saw as their natural abilities, which in turn led to a staggering increase in disparity in wealth between the best and worst well-off social groups. In the case of the United States the share of wealth controlled by the top 1% of the population increased from 22% in 1989 to 31% in 2025,[44] leaving the bottom 50% owning 2% in 2025.[45] In

[40] Emmer (2007).

[41] Henderson (2015).

[42] Mathew (2008).

[43] Heater (1999, pp. 26–7).

[44] Bhutada (2025).

[45] Rao (2025).

Australia the share of wealth held by the top 1% increased from 12% in 2002 to 24% in 2020, leaving the bottom 40% with 5.5%.[46]

Conservative commitment to property rights is also manifest in their rejection of the concept of socio-economic rights or the idea that the state has a role in remedying inequalities through the provision of welfare. This is grounded in the view that equality is incompatible with liberty because the furtherance of equality requires expenditure of public money raised through taxation, which conservatives characterise as an intrusion on the economic liberty of those who pay it.[47] As former Australian Treasurer Joe Hockey phrased it.[48]

> …the average working Australian, be they a cleaner, a plumber or a teacher, is working over one month full-time each year just to pay for the welfare of another Australian … it is not the role of government to use the taxation and welfare system as a tool to 'level the playing field' … We must reward the lifters and discourage the leaners.

In line with their defence of free enterprise, conservatives do not resent social mobility. They laud the 'self-made' person who overcomes a deprived background to become successful. However, they reject state assistance to overcome deprivation. As Heater explained, conservatives adopt[49]

> ..the key assertion that the underlying objective of social citizenship, namely the shaping of a more equal society, is a forlorn hope for the simple reason that people are inherently unequal: this fact of human nature should be accepted; the state should not try to tamper with it.

Each individual's success or failure thus depends on their own efforts—perhaps aided by private charity. Members of society do not owe obligations to their fellow citizens—as Margaret Thatcher said 'There is no such thing as society.'[50]

Why can conservatism be characterised as inimical to reason? Conservatives certainly deploy reason in constructing arguments in support of their policies—to take a random example, they will present a rationally constructed argument against welfare support by saying that that policy may (depending on the circumstances) require increased government borrowing and put upward pressure on interest rates. But the use of reason within the framework of conservative ideology is not the point—rather the issue is that the ideology is built upon a foundation that rejects the application of reason as a way of formulating an ethical code and of determining the balance between the individual and state. The degree to which conservatism is antithetical to reason in this sense is well illustrated by Burke's statement that prejudice is to be preferred to reason in decision-making, arguing that the former is superior because it is the product of life experience and tradition rather than abstract thought.[51] The use of devices such as Rawls' original position is therefore fundamentally incompatible with conservatism, because for conservatives values are not

---

[46] Basford Canales (2025), Katic and Leigh (2016).

[47] Nisbet (2002, pp. 60–1).

[48] Whiteford (2023).

[49] Heater (1999, p. 25).

[50] Kitching (2020, p. 566).

[51] Nisbet (2002, pp. 44–9).

arrived at through a process of reasoning but rather by historical observation of what 'works'—which, importantly, means what is conducive to order. It follows that there is no room within the conservative mindset for the idea that the institutions of state should be designed in accordance with fundamental principles such as those articulated by Rawls, that a constitution should guarantee civil and socioeconomic rights or that human dignity should be the fundamental value underpinning society. In its rejection of an ethic founded upon reason, conservatism is thus fundamentally antithetical to good citizenship.

2.2.4 Populism

In contrast to religion and conservatism, populism is not an ideology. It is a political practice founded on an appeal to public discontent arising from issues such as wealth inequality, governmental corruption, immigration and people's perception that they are voiceless. As Velasco states[52]

> ...populism is a way of doing politics in which 'the people' are pitted in conflict against others – various 'elites', local minorities, immigrants, foreigners...populism rests on a triad: denial of complexity, distrust of pluralism and anti-elitism.

Identification of a group, which can be defined by socio-economic class, ethnicity, migrant status or cultural values with which other voters can be placed in an antagonistic relationship is the cornerstone of populism which thrives on fear, resentment or disdain fomented against the group being targeted. Antagonism against the target group is often heightened by the claim that the group has been accorded some special status, for example under diversity programmes. Populism is 'a style of politics that manipulates and exacerbates identity cleavages for political gain...it is always an *us* against *them*'.[53] This reliance on an identification of an 'other' means that populists are often more sure of who they are not than who they are.[54] Sometimes populism will draw upon multiple social divisions, an example of which was Donald Trump's 2024 presidential campaign which exploited economic discontent, fear of migrants and cultural divisions over abortion and diversity.

As a methodology, populism transcends ideology, and in many instances, populist movements defy characterisation as being of the right or left—Peronism in Argentina being an example.[55] However, it is also true that because it is a method rather than an ideology, it has been used as a tool by both left and right. As Taggart states[56]

> The reason for its adaptability lies in the 'empty heart' of populism: populism lacks a commitment to key values. While ideologies contain, either implicitly or explicitly, a focus

[52] Velasco (2022, p 13).

[53] Velasco (2022, pp. 22–3).

[54] Taggart (2000, p. 94).

[55] Taggart (2000, pp. 61–6).

[56] Taggart (2000, pp. 3–4).

on one or more values such as equality, liberty and social justice, populism has no such core to it.

What populist platforms have in common is a promise to provide solutions to issues that voters believe have been disregarded by other parties. In many instances the 'solutions' would have catastrophic consequences. For example, economic analyses of populism may highlight the incompatibility between its promise to provide jobs, growth or income distribution (or combinations of these) and its disregard of consequential risks in the form of inflation and/or deficits.[57] Thus, former UK Prime Minister Tony Blair perceptively described populism as exploiting a grievance rather than solving it.[58] However to populists, failure to provide a solution is irrelevant because a thread common to all manifestations of populism is the primacy attached to the acquisition of power for its own sake.

Of course, it is true that all political parties seek to obtain power. But a number of characteristics serve to differentiate populists from other political movements: In contrast to parties with set positions, in many cases populist movements manifest an infinite flexibility when it comes to policy formulation—everything is directed towards identifying and exploiting voter discontent. This frequently leads to populist parties downplaying or concealing policies which risk alienating voters but which they intend to implement after gaining power.[59] As Taggart states 'Populism has an essentially chameleonic quality that means it always takes on the hue of the environment in which it occurs.'[60] Most concerningly however is the fact that, and again in contrast with other parties, populists frequently manifest only a qualified commitment to constitutionalism, which they adhere to in favourable circumstances but which is abandoned if constitutional restraints stand in the way of the acquisition of power or the implementation of policy. This often manifests itself in attacks on the judiciary and calls to 'take back control' from undemocratic judge-made law, an example of which from the UK was provided by an article by the editor of the *Daily Mail*, with the headline 'Enemies of the People' below photographs of judges who had found that parliamentary approval was needed for the country to leave the European Community.[61] A far more serious populist attack on the constitutional order was provided by the Capitol insurrection of 6 January 2021, which Donald Trump arguably incited and certainly did nothing to prevent,[62] and by the subsequent defence of the insurrection by elements within the Republican party. Similarly, in the Philippines, Rodrigo Duterte drew on widespread popular discontent with drug trafficking during his campaign for president, urging voters to kill both dealers and addicts. His subsequent tenure in office was marked by the extrajudicial killing of 30,000 people, which he is alleged to have both authorised and incentivised.[63] In this

[57] Dornbusch and Edwards (1991, p. 9).

[58] BBC (2024b).

[59] Mikucka-Wójtowicz (2019, p. 457).

[60] Taggart (2000, p. 4).

[61] Slack (2016).

[62] Ignatieff (2022, p. 38).

[63] Ratcliffe (2024).

way, populism may sometimes sit uncomfortably between constitutional parties and those which are obviously authoritarian, operating within the constitutional system while also being prepared to act outside of it.

A common characteristic of populist movements is the harnessing of public resentment of so-called 'elites' who are believed to have captured the institutions of government and to exercise power without regard to the interests of ordinary people. These elites are characterised as being both outside and on top of the rest of society and of not sharing the same views, values and culture as ordinary people on whom they wish to impose their views.[64] Populist parties promise to wrest control of government from the elite and to return it to the hands of the people—as represented, of course, by the populist party. To what extent is the charge of elitist capture of the state valid? The exercise of political power, other than that taking the form of voting, is inevitably conducted by elites in the sense that the effective running of government requires a degree of expertise gained in politics or some other area of endeavour. So characterising government as the preserve of an 'elite' is to state something that is unavoidable and obvious.[65] However, what is of legitimate concern is the circumstance where opportunities to participate in government are manipulated in such a way as to lead to it being dominated by a particular group. Here the charge of elitism is well-founded. Key factors which lead to this circumstance are the influence of money on elections to the extent that a group can effectively buy control over government, the growth in party discipline that prevents legislators from representing voters' interests and, perhaps most significant of all, electoral systems that fail to produce results that accurately reflect voter sentiment—factors that will be explored in Chap. 4.

But while accepting the legitimacy of popular concerns about elitism in the sense described above, the populist approach to elitism is profoundly cynical. Populist parties themselves rely for their success on the same factors—access to money and exploitation of the electoral system—as do other elites. This fact highlights one of the paradoxes of populism, which is that populists often succeed in harnessing anti-elitism in order to induce voters to support candidates whose policies are in reality inimical to the interests of the ordinary people populists claim to champion. An example of this was the support Donald Trump gained from economically marginalised voters in 2024, despite his having adopted tax policies that overwhelmingly favoured an elite comprised of wealthy individuals and corporations when in office between 2017 and 2021.[66] The reason for this was that for many voters, the opportunity to express defiance of the 'elites' (those who pointed to the social harm that would be caused by the reduction in taxes on the wealthy) by voting for a candidate mattered more than what that candidate did once in office. This example also reveals why it is a mistake to think of populism as a bottom-up movement acting

64 Rodríguez-Pose (2022, p. 87).

65 Ignatieff (2022, p, 42).

66 Gumbel (2025).

for the benefit of ordinary people against elites. It is rather a manifestation of voter manipulation by a different elite. As Bufacchi states[67]

> …populism is a top-down phenomenon, nothing more than covert elitism. Populism arises in the context of a clash between ruling elites: it is the articulation of a calculated political strategy used by one section of the elite to gain the upper hand on [sic] a different section of the elite. In the last analysis, populism can be explained in terms of the masses being instigated and manipulated by some members of the elite in the pursuit of their own interests.

Those who populists refer to as 'elites' go far beyond holders of political power and are commonly identified as people who have qualifications or expertise that ordinary people do not have and who draw on their expertise on expressing views contrary to populist policies. An illustration of this is provided by the Brexit referendum in the United Kingdom in 2016. The reason why warnings by economists of the consequences of leaving the EU failed to deter voters from supporting the Leave campaign was precisely because these warnings were given by experts—as pro-Leave politician Michael Gove stated 'people in this country have had enough of experts.'[68]

Why does populism pose a threat to reason and thus to good citizenship? The already noted antipathy that populists manifest towards experts is one obvious answer. Rejection of fact-based argument is clearly incompatible with reason. However, a more fundamental basis for the view that populism is antithetical to reason: As already noted, Aristotle identified πάθος (pathos—appeal to emotion), and λογος (logos—appeal to reason) as contrasting tactics used in the conduct of politics.[69] That distinction lies at the heart of understanding the threat posed by populism to good citizenship. The reliance of populism on emotion is well articulated by the following description of the strategy of the National Front in France:[70]

> The Front's appeal sprang not from logic, rather from the emotions of those who felt betrayed by the political establishment and sought a new champion whom they could imagine understood their everyday concerned. It depended on a lot of people feeling fed up, and, so long as that continued to be the case, could expect to play a big political role.

Because exploitation of emotion is key to populists' success, their interests necessitate that voters be diverted from engaging in rational analysis. Reasoned debate is anathema to parties whose campaigns rely on voters suspending their intellectual faculties. Their strategy therefore relies on distraction of voters, and the overwhelming of their critical faculties, by showmanship, inflammatory speeches, denigration of opponents and avoidance of substantive debate.

---

[67] Bufacchi (2023, p. 130).

[68] Reed (2023).

[69] Aristotle *On Rhetoric* 1.2.

[70] Fenby (2015, p. xxix).

2.3 Tolerance

Tolerance is a necessary corollary of reason because reason-based decision-making can function only if consideration is given to all points of view.[71] Tolerance is most commonly justified with reference to the sceptical epistemology advanced by John Stuart Mill in *On Liberty* in which he argued that that freedom to express ideas ought not to be suppressed because to do so would be to claim infallibility, stating that[72]

> ..the opinion which it is attempted to suppress by authority may possibly be true. Those who desire to oppress it, of course deny its truth; but they are not infallible. They have no authority to decide the question for all mankind, and exclude every other person from the means of judging. To refuse a hearing to an opinion because they are sure that it is false, is to assume that their certainty is the same thing as absolute certainty. All silencing of discussion is an assumption of infallibility.

and similarly that[73]

> To call any proposition certain while there is anyone who would deny its certainty if permitted, but who is not permitted, is to assume that we ourselves, and those who agree with us, are the judges of certainty, and judges without hearing the other side.

According to this theory, because it is always *possible* that truths discovered by human reason are in fact errors which, if one is allowed to challenge them, may be replaced by a new truth,[74] one can never say *conclusively* that one has attained truth. All one can say is that rational argument in which all voices can be heard maximises the chances of discovering truth. Conversely one can say that what current analysis indicates is true holds sway until someone deploys rational analysis to disprove it. This stands in contrast to the ideas of post-modernists, who reject rational analysis and deny the existence of truth. It follows, therefore, that answers to questions about truth are attainable only if there is freedom of thought, expression and inquiry.[75] It also follows that political questions must be answered with an acceptance of fallibility and without recourse to authority or force.[76]

This epistemological justification aside, tolerance is also important because of the positive effect it has on the political process. Tolerance requires that participants political debate with a willingness to at least contemplate changing their views if persuaded by objective evidence. Tolerance also requires people to view their political opponents' contributions to public debate as valuable and well-intentioned, rather than as being the product of evil or ignorance.[77] It is precisely the absence of tolerance that has led to increasing political polarisation, particularly in the United States.[78]

---

[71] Davies et al. (1999, p. 51).

[72] Mill (1859, p. 37).

[73] Mill (1859, p. 41).

[74] Schauer (1982, pp. 24–9).

[75] Smolla (1993, pp. 6–17).

[76] Bufacchi (2023, p. 118).

[77] Odermatt and Siscoe (2023, pp. 60–62).

[78] Persily (2015, pp. 4–7).

While polarisation in the sense of fervent attachment to competing opinions is an inevitable, and not necessarily negative, feature of politics, what has become evident is increasing incivility in politics[79] and a tendency of members of political blocs to view each other's members as worthless, treasonous and meriting hatred.[80] As a consequence, compromise and consensus-seeking have become virtually absent from the political landscape.[81] At its worst, intolerance leads to threats of violence such as those made against electoral officials,[82] and actual violence as manifested in the insurrection of 6 January 2021.[83] The problem becomes particularly challenging when reasoned argument by one side of a question is met with invective rather than counter-argument by the other, leading to an overall coarseness in debate as where invective and insult are substituted for reasoned argument.[84] At its worst, such behaviour descends into denigration and mockery of groups such as disabled people and ethnic minorities, which has become a feature of politics in the United States,[85] Australia[86] and the United Kingdom.[87]

Justification of freedom of expression, and thus of tolerance of opposing views, on the basis of truth-seeking is sound, but raises the question of whether tolerance should extend even to those propounding views that reject tolerance. Should the law of a society based on human dignity permit a political party to campaign on a platform of replacing the institutions of that society with a dictatorship? This question, referred to as the paradox of tolerance, has divided political philosophers. Popper took the view that a free society is entitled to suppress the expression of ideas antithetical to its values in order to protect itself from such ideas gaining electoral support.[88] By contrast Rawls stated that following that course would mean that a free society would no longer free and had adopted the values of those opposed to it. He did however distinguish the expression of opinions that were hostile to tolerance from conduct intended to overthrow a tolerant political order, from which conduct a free society could defend itself.[89] I would argue that Rawls' view is preferable both on the principled ground he advances as well as on the pragmatic ground that suppression of a viewpoint would drive it underground and would mean that it is not exposed to refutation in the marketplace of ideas. It would also cast the state in the role of determining what ideologies may and may not be propagated. As was stated by

79 Van't Riet and Van Stekelenburg (2022, p. 203).
80 Siscoe (2023).
81 Feldmann (2022).
82 Goudswand (2023).
83 Sherman (2024).
84 Leingang (2024).
85 Carmon (2016).
86 Smee (2019), Bolza (2024).
87 Mulholland (2011).
88 Popper (1966, pp. 265–6).
89 Rawls (1972, p. 220).

Jackson J in *West Virginia State Board of Education v Barnette*,[90] a case involving the free speech clause of the First Amendment in the United States:

> If there is any fixed star in our constitutional constellation, it is that no official, high or petty, can prescribe what shall be orthodox in politics, nationalism, religion or other matters of opinion...

Leaving aside theoretical justification of tolerance, its practice is important because of the positive effect it has on social relations, in particular in reducing the level of conflict in society. This is because tolerance is closely related to empathy—the capacity to see ourselves in others and to understand how they feel.[91] If people develop the capacity to recognise the commonality they share with others—including with their political opponents—the likelihood will increase that political questions will be decided on rational grounds, with tolerance for the views of others leading to answers based on the best arguments that each has to offer. Indeed, the evidence is that by displaying empathy for the views of one's opponents, one increases the likelihood of persuading them to accept one's own arguments.[92]

2.4 Public Participation

The discussion earlier in Chap. 1 showed that ancient civic republicanism placed as much emphasis on the duties attaching to citizenship as to the rights derived from it. A citizen was considered to be under a positive obligation to participate in public affairs. Moreover, in doing so they were to use their abilities for the common good and not purely in the pursuit of personal ambition or interests. However, recent decades have seen a decline in political engagement in many countries. In the United Kingdom this has manifested itself in declining electoral turnout along with non-involvement in activities such as political party membership, reading or watching media produced by parties or engagement in discussions with others about who to vote for.[93] Similarly in the United States there has been a decline in formal political engagement,[94] while in Australia, where voting, in the sense of a legal obligation to attend the polls and receive a ballot paper is mandatory, an indication of non-engagement is the fact that there has been a decline in membership of political parties over recent decades[95] and a 2024 survey revealed that only 37% of respondents in Australia were satisfied with democracy and 52% said that they had little or no interest in politics.[96]

It is concerning that many people do not appear to mind being uninformed about how they are governed or, even if they are, are not sufficiently interested to make

[90] 319 U.S. 624 (1943) 642.

[91] Brown (2021, pp. 120–2), Decety and Cowell (2015, pp. 3–4).

[92] Santos et al. (2022, pp. 1570–1).

[93] Uberoi and Johnston (2022, pp. 7–14).

[94] Putnam (2000, pp. 11–64), Macedo et al. (2005, p. 20).

[95] Davies (2020).

[96] Lewis (2024).

the effort to become informed, restricting their horizon to quotidian concerns and their own immediate interests. Yet even leaving aside principled reasons why people should become informed, active citizens, a pragmatic reason is that ultimately how government is conducted impacts upon their own personal interests in multiple ways, even if they do not realise that fact. Citizenship requires effort—the effort to think and the effort of becoming involved,[97] and it is the role of education in civics and citizenship to help people achieve this.

The reasons for lack of civic participation are varied. Key among them is the disillusionment felt by people in the way politics is conducted. In opinion surveys conducted in Australia,[98] the United Kingdom,[99] the United States[100] and many other countries[101] politicians are variously rated as dishonest, incompetent, out of touch with the concerns of ordinary people and motivated by short-term self-interest rather than the common good. However I would argue that a more fundamental cause of disillusionment than behaviour of individual politicians is systemic problems relating to how the institutions of the state are structured and how they operate. Underlying these problems is the fact that constitutions either do things inadequately or fail to do them at all. More attention will be focused on constitutions in Chaps. 4 and 5, but as an example of their failings, one can cite instances where, supposedly democratic constitutions permit elections to be conducted on the basis of single-member constituencies rather than mandating an electoral system that gives proportional results, which would achieve what one would think was a fundamental objective of a democratic system, which is to ensure that the composition of the legislature accurately reflects the support that parties have among voters.[102] Another example is the failure of constitutions to embody mechanisms which ensure that politicians are held to account for breaches of standards of behaviour or corruption.[103] In light of this, it is unsurprising voter disenchantment with public institutions has translated into a decline in willingness to engage in public affairs,[104] a trend which has the effect of increasing the lack of contact between politicians and the people they govern, which in turn increases public disillusionment with the political process.

Formal engagement in politics aside, participation in the broad sense can manifest itself in a variety of other ways, such as signing a petition, participating in an online campaign, attending a public demonstration or joining a union. All of these are properly considered examples of the practice of good citizenship, because they all contribute to the good of society. Research on political participation in the UK, France and Germany shows that whereas older people are more likely to participate

---

[97] Heater (1999, p. 73).

[98] Harris (2020, pp. 1–2).

[99] Butler (2024).

[100] Pew Research Centre (2023).

[101] Kehoe (2022).

[102] Harris (2020, pp. 63–71).

[103] Harris (2020, pp. 10–20).

[104] Keet (2019, p. 17).

in politics by voting, younger people are more likely to undertake these types of informal engagement.[105]

A method of participation that has attracted increasing attention is the use of deliberative assemblies in which randomly selected citizens convene to discuss a public issue, thereby enhancing their knowledge of public affairs and giving them practice at political participation.[106] Whereas many citizens think of their civic engagement as involving only the private act of casting of a vote following purely internal 'deliberation,' deliberation in the true sense involves citizens publicly interacting with each other, using reasoned argument to explain their views and testing them in light of the views of others in the belief that that will lead to more informed decision-making.[107] The process is also used in the hope that face to face interaction will lead to an increase in civility and counter the aggression that often characterises remote interactions on social media. Deliberation of this type parallels what happens in the jury room during a trial, the differences being that the issue being deliberated upon is political rather than legal. There have been notable instances where citizen assemblies have made a positive contribution to political decision-making. An example from New Zealand was the Citizens' Assembly convened to discuss how to secure Auckland's water supply and to provide recommendations to Watercare, the water company owned by the city council.[108] The Assembly process was notable for creating an environment in which participants were able to obtain an understanding of the complex science involved in water supply planning and for showing the benefits of consensus-based rather than adversarial democracy.[109] Examples from Canada are provided by the Citizens Assemblies held in British Columbia (2004) and Ontario (2006) which were convened to discuss options for a new electoral system for each province, with the option ultimately selected by the Assembly being put to voters in a referendum.[110] The success of a citizens' assembly depends on the design of the process by which invitations to participate are sent to citizens so as to ensure that the assembly is broadly reflective of the composition of the population, as well as the provision of adequate resources, such as compensation for expenses, accommodation and child care so as not to exclude people who would otherwise not be able to attend.[111]

Levels of participation depends not only on motivation to participate—which is a chiefly a function of attitude and interest—but also the capacity to participate. This requires not only a factual knowledge of how political processes work but also the ability to engage in critical thinking, which equips citizens with the intellectual tools needed to challenge structural shortcomings in the design of public institutions and the behavioural shortcomings in the way holders of public office exercise power.[112]

---

105 Melo and Stockemer (2014, pp. 45–8).

106 Peterson (2011, p. 102).

107 Petersen (2011, pp. 149–50), Samuelsson (2016, p. 2).

108 Buklijas et al. (2023).

109 University of Auckland (2025).

110 Pal (2012).

111 Fillet (2023).

112 Davies et al. (1999, pp. 57–8), Melo and Stockemer (2014, pp. 40–1).

Education on how to analyse issues from differing viewpoints, along with reinforcement of the view that each citizen's contributions are welcome and will serve as a contribution to society, are critical to the development of the fully engaged citizen and are further discussed in Chap. 3.

2.5 Kindness, Civility and Altruism

The final element of good citizenship covers a broad category of interpersonal behaviours, embracing kindness, civility and altruism. Earlier in this chapter we noted that among the duties which Cicero attached to good citizenship was that of acting with kindness towards others. Strictly legal conceptions of the duties owed by a citizen do not extend to imposing obligations in respect of modes of personal interaction unless a breach of the law is involved. Yet there is an increasing recognition that good citizenship in the broadest sense encompasses an obligation to act kindly towards others as an ethical duty.

Kindness is closely related to civility, best defined as the practice of acting with consideration towards others, for example by tolerating divergent views, addressing others courteously, respecting their privacy and taking care to put others at ease in the myriad of social interactions that one engages in.[113] Civility confers a direct benefit on public affairs, because people are more likely to contribute to public life if personal interactions—political debate included—are conducted in a civil manner. Conversely the absence of civility, which unfortunately characterises politics in many societies, deters political participation.[114]

Just as kindness and civility towards people are other-regarding behaviours, so too is altruism—the practice of acting for the benefit of others, even if at a cost to ones-self.[115] Like participation, altruism imposes a positive obligation on the citizen. Bellamy underscores the importance of 'good neighbourliness' arising from the fact that law on its own is an inadequate tool for ensuring ordered living and that therefore we have to rely on people acting well towards each other.[116] The difference between participation and altruism is that whereas participation relates to engagement in the political process with the aim of furthering one's own views, altruism involves a broader range of activities directed towards providing a benefit for others. The two may of course overlap, for example in the case of involvement in a political campaign directed towards the enhancement of the rights of a disadvantaged group.

Altruism requires a person to set aside the individualism which, although the cornerstone of autonomy and thus a value that supports human dignity will, if left unchecked, lead to a society where people perceive each other primarily in competitive and sometimes antagonistic terms and where social bonds become weakened.

---

113 Calhoun (2000, pp. 255–60).

114 Calhoun (2000, p. 266).

115 Bar-Tal (1986, pp. 4–7).

116 Bellamy (2010, p. xiii).

Teachers in the United Kingdom identified altruism and a willingness to act in the interests of others and not solely in one's own as a key element of good citizenship because it acts as a counter to the attitude that one should always seek to obtain an advantage over others and put ones-self first.[117] There is evidence that while altruistic conduct is primarily motivated by a desire to act for the benefit of others, some choose to devote their abilities and energy to altruism as a substitute for political engagement because they are disillusioned with politics.[118]

Engagement in voluntary activity builds social capital, by which is meant the capacity of people to work collaboratively and to trust each other.[119] In a society with high social capital, people feel empathy for each other and are more likely to help someone in need—which in turn makes the person who received assistance more likely to help someone-else. The result is that people come to expect empathetic treatment and to trust each other, which causes them to take on the obligation to act in similar fashion towards others. In addition to promoting social harmony, high levels of social capital lead to improved health, higher standards of education and, importantly for citizenship, enhanced political participation.[120] Private altruistic activity is consistent with civic republicanism, in that it increases harmony[121] which in turn affects the public sphere because it increases the likelihood that political questions will be decided by means of consensus-building rather than through binary antagonism—a common feature of those democracies dominated by two political blocs.[122] The outward-looking nature of altruism creates social bonds because it usually takes the form of activity that requires face to face interaction with others, in contrast to the increasing tendency of people to engage largely, and in some cases almost entirely, via social media, where lack of physical presence means that the impact of one's interactions on others is less apparent and where anonymity fosters lack of restraint.

Finally, the practice of altruism is, unfortunately, noteworthy for its absence in the conduct of many politicians. The idea of a politician acting contrary to their own interests seems, on the face of it, to be absurd. While office-seeking is sometimes motivated by a desire to effect change for the common good, one would be naïve not to recognise that in most instances it is the product of a desire to accumulate power. While a belief that one has the ability to govern is in itself not blameworthy, what is antithetical both to good citizenship and good government is acquisition and retention of power for its own sake, and an unwillingness to make decisions in the interest of society as a whole, even if at detriment to one's own interests. The implications of good citizenship for political leadership are explored in Chap. 6.

The positive effects of kindness, civility and altruism show that good citizenship has implications not only in the public sphere where people interact in their capacity as political actors constituting the most basic building block of the *res publica*, but

---

[117] Davies et al. (1999, p. 50).

[118] Henn et al. (2005, p. 3).

[119] Whiteley (2012, pp. 76–7).

[120] Halpern (2005, pp. 106–112, 166–9, 188–92).

[121] Peterson (2011, pp. 108–9).

[122] Harris (2020, p. 19).

also in the private sphere in their capacity as strangers, friends and family members engaging with each other in the course of day to day living.[123] Thus the practice of the elements of good citizenship—reason, tolerance, participation and the interpersonal behaviours of kindness, civility and altruism—confers benefits in all spheres of human existence.

References

Anderson S (2016) Peter Dutton suggests Fraser government made mistake by resettling Lebanese refugees. ABC News. Accessed 21 Nov 2016

Aristotle. On Rhetoric. Kennedy G (trans). Oxford University Press, New York

Bar-Tal D (1986) Altruistic motivation to help: definition, utility and operationalization. Humboldt J Soc Relat 13:3–14

Basford Canales S (2025) Share of wealth held by Australia's poorest falls sharply since 2004 – report. The Guardian. Accessed 13 Feb 2025

Bellamy R (2010) Introduction. In: Bellamy R and Palumbo A (eds) Citizenship. Ashgate Publishing, Farnham

BBC News (2024a) Trump repeats baseless claim about Haitian immigrants eating pets. Accessed 16 Sept 2024

BBC (2024b) Amal Rajan interviews Toby Blair. BBC. Accessed 4 Sept 2024

Bolza M (2024) Hanson tweet to Muslim senator 'ultimate racist slur'. The Canberra Times. Accessed 1 Nov 2024

Brown B (2021) Atlas of the heart. Vermilion, London

Bufacchi V (2023) Why Cicero matters. Bloomsbury, London

Bhutada G (2025) Visualized: the 1%'s Share of U.S. wealth over time (1989–2024). Visual capitalist. Accessed 8 Feb 2025

Buklijas T, Bardsley A, Allen K, Guy C, Wigley J, Ryan L (2023) Citizens' assembly on the next source of water for Tāmaki Makaurau Auckland - a case study of deliberative democracy in Aotearoa

Burke J (1790) Reflections on the revolution in France. James Dodsley, London

Butler P (2024) Trust in British politics hits record low, latest BSA survey finds. The Guardian Australia. Accessed 12 June 2024

Cassidy C, Rose T (2024) Sydney council bans same-sex parenting books from libraries for 'safety of our children'. The Guardian Australia. Accessed 7 May 2024

CBS News (2022) French President Emmanuel Macron calls for more respect on social media. Accessed 4 Dec 2022

Calhoun C (2000) The virtue of civility. Philos Public Aff 29:251–75

Carmon I (2016) Donald Trump's worst offense? Mocking disabled reporter, poll finds. NBC News. Accessed 11 Aug 2016

Davies A (2020) Party hardly: why Australia's big political parties are struggling to compete with grassroots campaigns. The Guardian Australia. Accessed 13 Dec 2020

Davies I, Gregory I, Riley S (1999) Good citizenship and educational provision. Taylor & Francis, London

Decety J, Cowell J (2015) Empathy, justice, and moral behavior. AJOB Neurosci 6:3–14

Donadio R (2021) What forces hold a liberal democracy together? What forces can tear a liberal democracy apart? The Atlantic, pp 72–8. Accessed Dec 2021

Dornbusch R, Edwards S (1991) The macroeconomics of populism. In: Dornbusch R, Edwards S (eds) The macroeconomics of populism in Latin America. University of Chicago Press, Chicago

[123] Calhoun (2000, pp. 251–75).

Emmer P (2007) The big disappointment. The economic consequences of the abolition of slavery in the Caribbean, 1833–1888. History in Focus 2007. https://archives.history.ac.uk/history-in-focus/Slavery/articles/emmer.html Accessed 23 April 2025
Feldmann L (2022) Big problems, consensus solutions: why so hard for congress to act? Christian science monitor. Accessed 31 May 2022
Fenby J (2015) The history of modern France from the revolution to the war on terror. Simon & Schuster, London
Fillet S (2023) Citizens' assemblies and panels on the rise: catching the deliberative wave. Go Vocal. Accessed 7 March 2023
Fulbrook M (2008) The People's State - East German Society from Hitler to Honecker. Yae University Press, New Haven
Goldberg M (2006) Kingdom coming: the rise of Christian nationalism. W.W. Norton, New York
Golec de Zavala A (2024) The psychology of collective narcissism – insights from social identity theory. Routledge, Abingdon
Goudswand A (2023) Georgia election worker 'terrorized' by threats after 2020 election. Reuters. Accessed 14 Dec 2023
Gumbel A (2025) 'There are a lot of bitter people here, I'm one of them': rust belt voters on why they backed trump again despite his broken promises. The Guardian. Accessed 11 Jan 2025
Halpern D (2005) Social capital. Polity Press, London
Hardaker D (2021) 'The Lord wants me to be prime minister' — how Scott Morrison foretold his destiny. Crikey. Accessed 3 Sept 2021
Harris B (2020) Constitutional reform as a remedy for political disenchantment in Australia – the discussion we need. Springer, Singapore
Heater D (1999) What is citizenship? Polity Press, Cambridge
Henderson A (2015) Government renews reservations about race discrimination ban in constitution ahead of indigenous recognition summit. ABC News. Accessed 4 July 2015
Henn M, Weinstein M, Forrest S (2005) Uninterested youth? Young people's attitudes towards party politics in Britain. Political Stud 53:1–24
Ignatieff M (2022) Democracy versus democracy: the populist challenge to liberal democracy. In: Velasco A, Bucelli I (eds) Populism - origins and alternative policy responses. LSE Press, London, pp 35–51
Karp P (2018) Peter Dutton says Victorians scared to go out because of 'African gang violence'. The Guardian Australia. Accessed 3 Jan 2018
Katic P, Leigh A (2016) Top wealth shares in Australia 2015–2012. The Rev Income Wealth 66(2014):209–222
Keet A (2019) Crisis and critique: critical theories and the renewal of citizenship, democracy, and human rights education. In: Zembylas M, Keet A (eds) Critical human rights, citizenship, and democracy education: entanglements and regenerations. Bloomsbury, London
Kehoe S (2022) Trust in government: a stark divide. Edelman trust. Accessed 20 Jan 2022
Kitching G (2020) No such thing as society: Thatcher, Wittgenstein and the philosophy of social science. The Econ Labour Relat Rev 31(2020):565–583
Kuntz M (2012) The postmodern assault on science. EMBO Rep 13:885–9
Leingang R (2024) Trump's bizarre, vindictive incoherence has to be heard in full to be believed. The Guardian Australia. Accessed 6 April 2024
Lewis P (2024) Australians are losing faith in democracy – most of us look at politics and recoil in horror or sullenly disengage. The Guardian. Accessed 16 July 2024
MacAskill E (2005) George Bush: 'God told me to end the tyranny in Iraq'. Guardian Australia. Accessed 7 Oct 2005
Macedo S, et al (2005) Democracy at risk: how political choices undermine citizen participation and what we can do about it. Brookings Institution Press, Washington
Marcos C (2024) Florida officials report hundreds of books removed from schools. The Guardian Australia. Accessed 13 Nov 2024

Martin S (2021) Scott Morrison tells Christian conference he was called to do God's work as prime minister. The Guardian Australia. Accessed 26 April 2021
Mason A (2007) Public justifiability, deliberation and civic virtue. Soc Theory Pract 33:679–700
Mathew P (2008) Black holes, white holes and worm holes: pre-emptive detention in the 'War on Terror'. In: Gani M, Mathew P (eds) Fresh perspectives on the 'War on Terror'. ANU Press, Canberra, pp 159–87
Melo D, Stockemer D (2014) Age and political participation in Germany, France and the UK: a comparative analysis. Comparative Eur Politics 33–53
Mikucka-Wójtowicz D (2019) The chameleon nature of populist parties. How recurring populism is luring 'the People' of Serbia and Croatia. Europe-Asia Stud 71:450–479
Mill JS (1859) On Liberty. Gray J and Smith G (eds) (1991). Routledge, London
Merriam-Webster Dictionary (online, 14 March 2025) 'citizenship.'
Morris N (2013) Ukip leader Nigel Farage puts threat of immigrant crime wave at centre stage for European elections. The Independent. Accessed 20 Sept 2013
Morrison S (2024) Plans for your good – a prime minister's testimony of god's faithfulness. W Publishing, Nashville
Mulholland H (2011) Charity voices anger after MPs 'mocked Tory with disability'. The Guardian. Accessed 8 Feb 2011
Nisbet R (2002) Conservatism- dream and reality. Transaction Publishers, New Brunswick
Nogrady B (2024) Harassment of scientists is surging. how should institutions respond? Nature 629:748–50
Odermatt Z, Ciscoe R (2023) Philosophical dialogue and the civic virtues: modeling democracy in the classroom. Anal Teach Philos Praxis 43:59–77
Oreskes N, Conway E (2022) From anti-government to anti-science: why conservatives have turned against science Deadalus 151:98–123
Pal M (2012) The promise and limits of citizens' assemblies: deliberation, institutions and the law of democracy. Queen's Law J 38:259–94
Persily B (2015) Introduction. In: Persily N (ed) Solutions to political polarization in America. Cambridge University Press, New York
Peterson A (2011) Civic republicanism and civic education: the education of citizen. Palgrave Macmillan UK, Houndmills
Pew Research Centre (2023) Americans' dismal view of the nation's politics. Pew Research Centre, Washington DC
Popper K (1966) The open society and its enemies – volume 1 – the spell of Plato. Routledge & Keegan Paul, London
Putnam (2000) Bowling alone – the collapse and revival of the American community. Simon & Schuster, New York
Rao P (2025) A visual breakdown of who owns America's wealth. Visual Capitalist. Accessed 4 March 2025
Ratcliffe R (2024) Rodrigo Duterte's 'war on drugs' in the Philippines – explained in 30 seconds. The Guardian. Accessed 4 Nov 2024
Rawls J (1972) A theory of justice. Clarendon Press, Oxford
Reed C (2023) Why so many people have had enough of experts – and how to win back trust. The Conversation. Accessed 29 June 2023
Reilly A (2019) Peter Dutton is whipping up fear on the medevac law, but it defies logic and compassion. The Conversation. 25 June 2019.
Rodríguez-Pose (2022) The rise of populism and the revenge of places that don't matter. In: Velasco A and Bucelli I (2022) Populism - origins and alternative policy responses. LSE Press, London, pp 79–103
Rozin P, Royzman E (2001) Negativity bias, negativity dominance, and contagion. Personality Soc Psychol Rev 5:296–320
Salam E and Pengelly M (2024) Texas approves new Bible-based curriculum for elementary schools. The Guardian Australia. Accessed 23 Nov 2024

Samuelsson M (2016) Education for deliberative democracy: a typology of classroom discussions. Democracy Educ 1:1–9

Santos L, Voelkel J, Willer R, Zaki J (2022) Belief in the utility of cross-partisan empathy reduces partisan animosity and facilitates political persuasion. Psychol Sci 33:1557–73

Sarup M (1993) An introductory guide to post-structuralism and postmodernism, 2nd edn. Harvester Wheatsheaf, Hemel Hempstead

Scott N, Seglow J (2007) Altruism. McGraw-Hill Education, Maidenhead

Schauer F (1982) Free speech: a philosophical inquiry. Cambridge University Press, Cambridge

Shapiro I (2024) Uncommon sense. Yale University Press, New Haven

Shepherd T (2024) How good are memoirs? In his testimony to Christian faith, Scott Morrison talks to God and God talks back. The Guardian. Accessed 3 May 2024

Sherman A (2024) Here's how election officials have boosted security since 2020's threats of violence. PBS News. Accessed 26 Oct 2024

Sisco W (2023) Race, gender, and the civic virtues: creating a flourishing society. Prindle Post. Accessed 2 Oct 2023

Slack J (2016) Enemies of the people. The Daily Mail. Accessed 4 Nov 2016

Smee B (2019) Peter Dutton condemned for 'disability excuse' slur against Ali France. The Guardian Australia. Accessed 12 April 2019

Smolla R (1993) Free speech in an open society. Vantage Books, New York

Sullivan M (2024) JD Vance is factually challenged – and morally deficient. The Guardian. Accessed 19 Sept 2024

Syal R (2023) Does Suella Braverman have evidence to link boat arrivals to crime? The Guardian Australia. Accessed 27 April 2023

Taggart P (2000) Populism. Open University Press, Buckingham

The Economist (2020). What is French laïcité?: The economist explains. The Economist. Accessed 23 Nov 2020

Tiwari P (2024) Donald Trump Shares video claiming god chose him to be "America's Caretaker". NDTV World. Accessed 16 Jan 2024

Uberoi E and Johnston N (2022) Political disengagement in the UK: who is disengaged? House of Commons Library, Westminster

University of Auckland (2025) Ordinary people, real power: can democracy be more democratic? University of Auckland, Auckland. Accessed 28 April 2025

Van't Riet J and Van Stekelenburg A (2022) The effects of political incivility on political trust and political participation: a meta-analysis of experimental research. Human Commun Res 48:203–29

Velasco A (2022) Populism and identity politics. In: Velasco A and Bucelli I (eds) Populism - origins and alternative policy responses. LSE Press, London, pp 9–34

Villareal A (2024) Trump's 'migrant crime' idea is vicious and legal immigrants could suffer. The Guardian. Accessed 8 Dec 2024

Wall S (2016) The pure theory of public justification. Soc Philos Policy 32:204–26

Wallis J, Hollyday J (eds) (1989) Crucible of fire: the church confronts apartheid. Orbis Books, Maryknoll

Washington H (2011) Climate change denial – heads in the sand. Earthscan, London

Whiteford P (2023) The welfare myth of 'lifters' and 'leaners' must be put behind us so robodebt is never repeated. The Sydney Morning Herald. Accessed 23 July 2023

Whiteley P (2012) Political participation on Britain – the decline and revival of civic culture. Palgrave Macmillan, Basingstoke

Chapter 3
Civics and Citizenship Education

Abstract The degree to which people are both capable and willing to be good citizens depends on the quality of the education they have received in civics and citizenship. The distinction between the two is important: In the context of education, civics refers to knowledge of the workings of the institutions of government. By contrast, citizenship refers to an understanding of the values underlying society. In many countries, inadequacies in the education system means that levels of knowledge of civics and citizenship are very low. This chapter discusses the principles that should underlie an effective system of civics and citizenship education, starting with the most fundamental principle which, consistent with the practice of reason, is that it should be founded on a secular ethic. A prime example of this is the *Enseignement Moral et Civique* (EMC—Moral and Civic Education) curriculum in France, which is based on the concept of *laïcité*, or secularism, and which is accompanied by a mandatory course in philosophy. An effective civics education programme should also extend throughout a student's school career, with complexity graded according to the stage a student has reached. The chapter ends by addressing the question of how effective civics knowledge is in giving people greater understanding of how government works, and of increasing their willingness to contemplate reform where needed. In doing so it analyses the results of a survey of voters conducted in Australia in 2025 which tested respondents' levels of civics knowledge and also presented them with a number of reform proposals, first without background information and again after providing information explaining the constitutional effect of the reforms. The results indicated that respondents demonstrated an increased willingness to support reform once furnished with accurate information about their effect, demonstrating the positive effect that civics education can have.

3.1 Levels of Civics Knowledge

Are education systems providing students with an adequate level of knowledge of civics and citizenship? A significant obstacle in the way of answering this question is that there is no set of data that measures knowledge of civics across a wide number

B. Harris, *Cultivating Good Citizenship*,
SpringerBriefs in Law, https://doi.org/10.1007/978-981-92-2740-2_3

of jurisdictions. The International Association for the Advancement of Educational Achievement (IEA) conducts periodic International Civic and Citizenship Education Study (ICCS) surveys testing the knowledge of Grade 8 (13–14 year-old) students. However, the most recent survey, conducted in 2022, was limited to 21 European countries along with Brazil, Colombia and Taiwan.[1] The scale against which student performance is measured provides results of limited usefulness, in that it consists of four levels of proficiency which are relatively easy to satisfy and not well differentiated.[2] More informative is recent data from the United States and Australia which have conducted recent surveys using questionnaires that test knowledge of the specifics of their constitutional systems.

In the United States the 2022 National Assessment of Educational Progress (NAEP) survey of the civics knowledge of 8th Grade students (aged 13–14) showed that only 22% of students met the 'proficient' standard, 48% met the 'basic' standard and 31% were 'below basic.'[3] Here it is important to note that the 'basic' standard means that a student has acquired only a 'partial mastery of prerequisite knowledge and skills', which NAEP states is not the desired goal.[4]

In Australia a 2015 survey found that only 65% of Australians knew that the country has a constitution—a lower proportion than in 1992.[5] The results of school examinations in 2024 showed that only 28% of Year 10 (16 year old) students were proficient in civics, the lowest rate recorded since the Australian Curriculum Authority began collecting data in 2004 and a decrease of 10% as compared to results from 2019.[6] A 2025 survey of Australians of voting age found that 51% said that they had bever been taught how the Constitution works, which suggests either that schools are not including civics and citizenship in the curriculum or that it is not making sufficient impact to enable students to recall it when they become adults.[7] 52% of respondents were unaware of the fact that the Constitution protects several fundamental rights. A week before a referendum held in 2023 on whether Australia's constitution should be amended to establish an advisory body representing the views of Indigenous people, many voters manifested high levels of disengagement from the process, stating either that they did not know that there would be a referendum or that they did not understand what the referendum was about.[8] This was despite the fact that the referendum had been preceded by a decade of public inquiries, that the campaign itself had lasted for 10 months, and that both the text of the proposal and the arguments on both sides were relatively easy to comprehend, requiring far less breadth of understanding than a general election in which there are multiple issues at play.

---

[1] International Association for the Advancement of Educational Achievement (2022).

[2] International Association for the Advancement of Educational Achievement (2022, pp. 65–8).

[3] National Assessment of Educational Progress (2022).

[4] Stedman (2011, p. 47).

[5] Miller (2015).

[6] Australian Curriculum, Assessment and Reporting Authority (2025, p. 19).

[7] The survey results are on file with the author.

[8] Rachwani (2023).

A 2025 report on civics education by the Australian Parliament's Joint Standing Committee on Electoral Matters, found that[9]

> ...many young people leave school without the knowledge and skills necessary to actively participate in Australian democracy, engage with civic practices and institutions, or understand basic processes like how to enrol to vote and cast a ballot correctly.

A number of factors could contribute to the low levels of civics knowledge in Australia, in particular the fact that insufficient attention is devoted to it in the curriculum, as is discussed in part 3 of this chapter. More significant, however, is the fact—scarcely credible but true nonetheless—that many politicians in Australia, particularly those from the dominant Liberal-National and Labor blocs, discourage voters from acquiring knowledge about the constitution. The reason for this is that the major parties benefit from structural defects in the constitution. This creates an incentive on the part of politicians to keep voters in a state of constitutional illiteracy, because the less voters know about the constitution, the more likely they are to vote against constitutional change. The role of politicians in undermining the civic development of voters is discussed in Chap. 5.

3.2 A Secular Ethic as the Foundation of Civics and Citizenship Education

Constitutional lawyers predictably focus on constitutional texts and the rules they contain which regulate interaction between the institutions of state. Yet the mechanics of a constitution are merely a reflection of the values that underlie it. It follows that the teaching of values must necessarily form the foundation of the curriculum. This highlights the importance of the distinction, discussed in Chap. 1 between civics (which relates to the mechanics of a constitution) and citizenship (which relates to the values that underly a constitution). Chapter 1 also discussed the meaning of 'good' in the phrase 'good citizenship,' arguing that unless one determines what 'goodness' is, it is impossible to take the subsequent step of determining what the practice of good citizenship entails.

Previously, education in values at schools was the preserve of religious bodies. The evident unsuitability of education based on faith rather than reason, along with the necessity of moral education as a key aspect of human development, makes it imperative that the educational system includes within its curriculum a secular system of values. As argued in Chap. 1, this should be founded upon the concept of respect for human dignity and all that that entails. The teaching of values should also encompass education in the practice of good citizenship which, as discussed in Chap. 2, embraces reason, toleration, engagement and empathy, in order to produce citizens who know not only the ethical theory underlying what makes a good citizen but also how to live as one. I would go further and argue that values education necessarily extends

---

[9] Commonwealth of Australia (2025, p. 39).

beyond values applied in the public sphere and encompasses the personal—what some commentators refer to as character education.[10] These include values such as truth, justice, honesty, kindness, perseverance and self-control.[11]

In some educational systems, both civics and citizenship education has been subsumed into personal, social and health education[12] However there is a good argument in favour of the opposite—that personal behaviour education should be taught as a dimension of civics and citizenship,[13] in line with the views of Aristotle and Cicero that being a good citizen and being a good person are mutually supportive concepts.[14] As Peterson states in commenting on one strand of modern civic republicanism[15]

> From this republican position, pupils must be educated to be a particular *type* of citizen: one able to act and participate effectively in public affairs, precisely because he possesses the necessary dispositions in his character.

In an era when the so-called 'culture wars' divide societies, the idea of values-based citizenship education will predictably encounter the charge that such a process would amount to indoctrination. There are a number of counter-arguments to that and in support of values to be taught by the public education system. Writing of the importance of values education to citizenship Heater states[16]

> Citizens need knowledge and understanding of the social, legal and political system(s) in which they live and operate. They need skills and aptitudes to make use of that knowledge and understanding. And they need to be endowed with values and dispositions to put their knowledge and skills to beneficial use.

First, it is naïve to expect values and an understanding of good citizenship to be innate. It is also clear that society cannot leave citizenship education to parents, just as it cannot leave the teaching of chemistry, history, psychology or mathematics to them. Professionalism is no less necessary in citizenship education than it is in any other area of the curriculum. Besides, the politicians who currently hold office reflect the values of those who elect them. If, to take Australia as an example, politicians engage in blatant misallocation of public funds through pork barrelling,[17] and conduct campaigns of sexist bullying in the corridors of parliament[18] one must conclude that there is a problem with the ethical standards of the adults in who elected those politicians and are responsible for the upbringing of future generations. Values therefore have to be formally taught via the education system. As Whiteley

[10] Oldfield (1990, pp. 164–5).
[11] Lickona (2004, pp. 7–11).
[12] Jerome et al. (2022. p. 9).
[13] Peterson (2011, pp. 135–6).
[14] Lu (2024, pp. 5–6, 11–12).
[15] Peterson (2011, p. 92).
[16] Heater (1999, p. 164).
[17] Harris (2024).
[18] Karvelas (2018).

states, 'for democracy to work, its citizens must have a combination of values and attitudes which are supportive of democratic politics.'[19] According to Plato what was necessary was[20]

> ...education from childhood in virtue, a training which produces a keen desire to become a perfect citizen who knows how to rule and be ruled as justice demands.

It is only if the values underlying good citizenship become what de Tocqueville referred to as 'habits of the heart'[21] that they will take root.

Second, it is naïve to think that *not* teaching values preserves ideological neutrality. In the absence of having been taught values, people will not be value-less—they will, by default, adopt values prevalent in society. Self-evidently every constitutional system is based on a set of values which, if not explicitly articulated in it will be evident from the way in which the constitution distributes and limits power. That set of values thus constitutes the country's official ideology. So there is nothing revolutionary in admitting that such an ideology exists. Indeed, the formulation of such an ideology, or adoption of the default one, is an inescapable choice. A decision not to teach values would therefore not be ideologically neutral—instead it would amount to leaving the ethical development of young people to be determined in accordance with whatever value-system has emerged as a result of the interplay of prevailing societal forces as they are from time to time. This idea that education on values amounts to indoctrination is therefore incorrect. People will always be exposed to values, the question is how to ensure that those values are ones that have been formulated in accordance with a process of reasoning, rather than those framed by the changing, and often unreasoning, prejudices of society.

Third, indoctrination refers to a process in terms of which[22]

> questions are suppressed rather than answered; whenever certain areas of questioning are taboo; and whenever the educator is psychologically unable to tolerate the expression of dissenting views.

Indoctrination involves the dissemination of material without regard for justifying evidence in order to instil unchallengeable dogmatic beliefs.[23] If indoctrination has been successful, a person who has been subject to it will be unwilling even to entertain alternatives, irrespective of evidence that might be presented in their favour. Indoctrination thus ultimately leads to a surrender of the will. Education in citizenship which has respect for human dignity at its core, and advocates the practice of reason, tolerance, participation and altruism, cannot be equated with indoctrination because those values are inconsistent with the practice of indoctrination as defined. The use of the techniques required for indoctrination would be self-defeating, as their incompatibility with the values being taught would signal that those values were not

[19] Whiteley (2012, p. 10).

[20] Plato *The Laws* 1.643.

[21] De Tocqueville (1835, p. 355).

[22] Cohen (1969, p. 180).

[23] Hoggan-Kloubert (2023, pp. 30–3).

espoused by the educator. The role of the citizenship educator is to present the values and practices of good citizenship and the reasoning underlying them, but ultimately it will be the choice of those being educated as to whether they accept them or not, or even adopt values that are antithetical to ones that have been taught. That is an inevitable risk that must be borne by a free society.[24] On the other hand, citizenship educators should not be diffident—as indicated in Chap. 2, many countries are experiencing a cultural conflict between those who espouse reason-based values and those who do not, and it is the role of the educator to explain why the method for arriving at the former is correct, why unreason poses a threat to society and what the consequences are if human dignity is not respected. There is no such thing as a value free world or a value free educational system. To repeat what was stated earlier, the inescapable question is what values will be absorbed by young people and how.

Finally, the process of education needs to be life-long.[25] Citizenship involves a mutuality of obligations binding the state, the citizen and citizens to each other. Among these obligations is the duty of citizens to uphold the concept of good citizenship itself. As Bellamy states[26]:

> Citizenship is a condition of civic equality. It consists of membership of a political community where all citizens can determine the terms and benefits of social cooperation on an equal basis. This status not only secures equal rights to the enjoyment of collective goods provided by the political association but also involves equal duties to promote and sustain them – including the good of democratic citizenship itself.

Therefore, successful cultivation of good citizenship requires that opportunities for education continue to be afforded to people throughout their lives.

3.3 The Content of the Civics and Citizenship Curriculum

3.3.1 Citizenship—The Values Foundation

If the teaching of values is to form the foundation of civics and citizenship education, how should that be realised in the curriculum?

Values education in the broadest sense consists of two strands. The first is teaching the intellectual skills needed to be an effective and engaged citizen—the capacity to engage in logical reasoning and to analyse and compare value systems. In practical terms this requires that the curriculum includes an introduction to philosophy, focussing on logic, ethics, and different schools of political theory.[27] The centrality

[24] Callan (1997, pp. 9–10).

[25] Schuller (2001, pp. 90–9).

[26] Bellamy (2010, p. xix).

[27] Pring (2001, p. 84).

of education on philosophical method to the development of good citizenship is concisely put by Bufacchi[28]:

> Democracy is not just an institutional system; it is also a culture. To strengthen democracy, one needs not only the right laws, one also needs the right form of political education. Unfortunately, culture takes time and effort. Developing a democratic culture is a slow process, requiring a lot of patience and a good dose of toleration. Deliberation is essentially what democracies are essentially about, and the process of deliberation involves taking time to listen to others, to evaluate their arguments, to ponder before civilly responding – all the skills that define sound philosophical engagement. The philosophical method is indistinguishable from the democratic method.

This aspect of the curriculum requires a level of intellectual development that students will reach only in the later years of secondary education, but the foundations can be laid in primary school through the inclusion of basic concepts such as the difference between right and wrong and the obligations to be considerate towards others and to avoid causing harm.

The second element of values education would focus specifically on the concept of human dignity as the value underlying good citizenship. This would draw on Rawls' methodology for an understanding of how the liberty and quality principles—which are implied by human dignity—are objectively arrived at, and would then apply those principles to contemporary issues. In doing this, teachers could run a Rawlsian simulation, in which students are allocated post-exercise identities known only to the teacher, placed behind the veil of ignorance and asked to devise fundamental rules of a society. A more specific exercise would be to agree on the contents of a bill of rights along with the test for determining when limitations of rights should be permitted. After this, students' post-exercise identities would be revealed to them and they would then be asked to comment on whether they felt that their interests would be adequately protected under the rules they had agreed.

In later years students would use the principles to critique their country's constitution to determine the extent to which it was consistent with human dignity and, where not, to suggest how it might be improved. This requires that students be taught the practical steps involved in critical reasoning,[29] with the object of fostering critical civic literacy, defined by Teitelbaum as follows[30]:

> Adopting a critical stance means not taking for granted what is known and in place, instead rigorously and wholeheartedly questioning the assumptions that undergird current ideas, practices, policies and structures.

In many countries the civics and citizenship curriculum presents the constitution as an eternal and immutable, rather than as being the product of its times and subject to change. It is unfortunately the case that, particularly in jurisdictions such as the United States and Australia where constitutional amendment is procedurally difficult, it is thought not worthwhile to discuss constitutional reform or invite students to

---

[28] Bufacchi (2023, p. 115).

[29] Lazere (2011, pp. 210–11).

[30] Teitelbaum (2011, p. 12).

contemplate what might be. Yet that attitude means that denial of the possibility of social progress becomes self-fulfilling. I would argue that cultivating in students the habit of questioning creates the best chance that they will effect change when, as adults, they become full participants in the political process. As will be discussed in Chap. 4, constitutional reform that enhances the protection of human rights, that makes the electoral system more representative and that increases the accountability of the government is likely to increase citizen participation in public affairs.

The values part of the curriculum would highlight the connection between the liberty, equality and civic republicanism which, as discussed in Chaps. 1 and 2, places importance on both individual liberty and the communitarian obligation to become an active citizen and, in so doing, to further the common good.[31] As Petersen states[32]

> Communitarian models of civic education prompt schools to consider the importance of teaching young people about their obligations to the community and to the common good, largely through service to their communities. Also central to communitarian civic education programmes is the development of character traits that can also be formed and expressed by providing pupils with the opportunity to learn in community settings.

Education on the communitarian aspect of civic republicanism will also foster in students a sense of belonging and of the bonds they have with fellow students as members of a shared political community.[33]

Another important element of values education is the fostering of deliberation which, as discussed in Chap. 2, is the practice by which citizens deploy reason and practice tolerance in making political choices. Reason-based decision-making is fundamental to the practice of good citizenship. It serves to counter decision-making based on emotion and inoculates voters against populist appeals that rely on voters suspending their capacity to reason. Training in the practice of deliberation, encompassing internal reflection, the capacity to distinguish fact from opinion, commitment to dialogue, communication skills (both speaking and listening) and empathy for the views of others as members of a shared community[34] should be included in the citizenship curriculum.[35] There are examples from a number of countries of how deliberation can be taught through practical classroom exercises.[36]

Despite its centrality to understanding values, philosophy appears as a mandatory part of the curriculum in relatively few countries.[37] Greatest attention is paid in France, where all students from first grade to the end of secondary school are taught values of freedom, equality and *laïcité* (secularism) that underlie the republic.[38]

---

[31] Peterson (2011, p. 148).

[32] Peterson (2011, p. 13).

[33] Peterson (2011, p. 123).

[34] Peterson (2011, pp. 136–43).

[35] Mason (2007, p. 679).

[36] Samuelsson (2016, pp. 4–8), Smith et al. (2021).

[37] Examples being France, Finland, Spain, Italy, Portugal, Germany, Switzerland and Sweden. See Le Roux (2011) and Humphreys (2013).

[38] Donadio (2021, p. 74), Johnson and Morris (2012, pp. 290–1).

The importance of values in the curriculum is indicated by the name of the civics subject: *Enseignement Moral et Civique* (EMC—Moral and Civic Education). The curriculum is based on civic republicanism and is directed towards instilling in students a sense of civic virtue—that is recognition that they are members of a community united in acceptance of republican values. Civic republicanism is also reflected in the fact that the curriculum emphasises the obligation of becoming an active citizen who participates in public life. In addition to studying civics, students are required to take a mandatory year-long philosophy subject in the final year of school, the object of which is stated as being to produce active citizens who have developed the intellectual capacity required to work out their own opinions rather than uncritically to accept the views of others.[39]

Values are also central to civics and citizenship education in Finland, which continues through all years 12 of school, which includes the study of philosophy in the final two years, and which is based on the view that 'education should begin with teaching universal values, like human rights and respect.'[40] The civics curriculum, which occupies 16% of class time in high school and evinces a high degree of congruence with civic republicanism. As Chen notes[41]

> According to the curriculum syllabus, Finnish students in grades one through five focus on four core content areas, the first being "human relations and ethical growth." Teachers lead students in discussing what empathy means, how to differentiate right from wrong, what friendship means, how to realize justice in daily life, whether wealth or poverty influences one's judgment of what is just, what the meaning of freedom of thought is, what religious freedom means, how to practice tolerance and how to refrain from discrimination.
>
> The second core content area is "self-identity and cultural identity." Here, teachers prompt students to ask themselves who they are, what they are capable of, who close to them comes from a different cultural or life background, what the characteristics of Finnish culture are, what the characteristics of the world's remaining ancient civilizations are, and what different beliefs and life philosophies are extant in various countries throughout the world.
>
> Finnish ethics classes also seek to imbue elementary school students with "concepts of human rights and a sense of community."

In England although the National Curriculum requires that students be taught critical thinking, as well as the concept of respect for people of different identities, there is no mention in of the teaching of values, philosophy or political ideology to which critical thinking could be applied.[42] However, legislation requires schools to 'promote the spiritual, moral, mental and physical development' of students.[43] In accordance with this, albeit using slightly different phraseology, the Department of Education requires schools to promote the 'spiritual, moral, social and cultural (SMSC) development' of students, stating that this encompasses a requirement to promote 'fundamental British values,' identified as 'democracy, the rule of law, individual liberty, and

[39] Mansfield (2023).

[40] Chen (2011).

[41] Chen (2011).

[42] Department of Education (2014a, pp. 82–4).

[43] Section 78(1)(a) of the *Education Act 2002* (UK).

mutual respect and tolerance of those with different faiths and beliefs.'[44] The National Curriculum to some extent reflects the influence of civic republicanism in that it includes education on how students can become active citizens who make a positive contribution to the community.[45] One can therefore say that while values are taught and the curriculum requires the development of critical thinking, in contrast to France there is no linking of the two through the teaching of philosophy.

In Australia the curriculum appears on the face of it to manifest a commitment to active citizenship and ethical understanding. The *Melbourne Declaration on Educational Goals for Young Australians*[46] laid out the goals for education in the twenty-first century. Goal 2 stated that students should be able to become 'successful learners, confident and creative individuals, and active and informed citizens.' The Declaration further stated that active and informed citizens 'are committed to national values of democracy, equity and justice, and participate in Australia's civic life' and 'work for the common good.' Despite this, the curriculum as implemented has been criticised for its focus on rote-learning of information about the institutions of government and its neglect of coverage of other countries' systems or of political ideologies and critical thinking.[47] The consequence is that the curriculum can lead to a 'non-critical understanding and assessment of what democracy is, and what it should be.'[48] The curriculum also fails to help students develop an ethical framework, despite the fact that one of the general capabilities that it requires is Ethical Understanding.[49] This begs the question as to how this can be achieved unless students are exposed to philosophy. As Henderson states[50]

> Of all the learning areas in the curriculum, civics and citizenship is uniquely placed to provide opportunities for young people to develop their ideals, values, morals and ethics as individuals and as members of society, and to learn how to act in accordance with them in various contexts.

In a paper drafted to guide development of the curriculum[51] the Australian Curriculum and Assessment and Reporting Authority stated that

> The values on which Australia's democracy is based include freedom of the individual, government by the people through a representative parliament, free and fair elections, the rule of law, equality of all before the law, social justice and equality, respect for diversity and difference, freedom of speech and religion, lawful dissent, respect for human rights, support for the common good, and acceptance of the rights and responsibilities of citizenship.

It is naïve to think that students can properly understand the meaning of concepts such as 'democracy' and 'freedom' without some prior knowledge of political philosophy.

---

[44] Department of Education (2014b).

[45] Department of Education (2014a, p. 3).

[46] United Nations (2010).

[47] Commonwealth of Australia (2025, pp. 28–31).

[48] Zyngier (2012).

[49] Australian Curriculum, Assessment and Reporting Authority (2019).

[50] Henderson (2017, p. 42).

[51] Australian Curriculum, Assessment and Reporting Authority (2012, p. 5).

Yet there is no recognition in the curriculum that the meaning of these concepts ultimately depends upon values, that their content is contested and that in certain circumstances they may clash—a clash which can be resolved only through the application of value-based judgements. There is irony in the fact that whereas Australia is one of the few jurisdictions where voting is compulsory—a legislative choice that is consistent with civic republicanism—it fails to provide its citizens with either an understanding of their system of government or the intellectual capacity to analyse political issues that civic republicanism requires. This is no better illustrated than by the 2023 constitutional referendum on an Indigenous advisory body, which was characterised by widespread voter disinterest and an inability to understand the relatively simple proposal put before them, factors which created the opportunity for opponents of the proposal to disseminate misinformation and to rely on the slogan 'If you don't know, vote no' which, with its implied validation of voters not taking steps to inform themselves, was the antithesis of civic republicanism.

3.3.2 *Civics—The Institutions of Government*

The second element of the curriculum consists of civics—instruction on the institutions of government. Fundamental to this is an understanding of the doctrine of constitutionalism, which is that the powers of the state should be defined and limited by law. The effectiveness of limits on state power requires adherence to what in common law countries is termed the rule of law, which among other things requires that the political organs—the legislature and executive—comply with decisions by the courts in cases where the legality of state actions are challenged. The rule of law can be contrasted with its antithesis—arbitrary government—where the state acts purely in accordance with its political interests, unconstrained by legal rules. However a shortcoming of the rule of law doctrine is that, as traditionally understood it requires only that government operates by law rather than by arbitrary will, that law is made by a defined process, that the content of the law is publicly ascertainable, that the law applies to everyone equally and that it is enforced by independent courts.[52] Although there is a line of thought that the meaning of the doctrine should be broadened so as to include a requirement that the *content* of the law comply with an external standard of justice,[53] many countries which proclaim adherence to the rule of law do so without any constitutional restraint in the competence of the legislature.

Broader than the rule of law is the *Rechtsstaat* or 'state-under-law' principle which originates in Germany and forms the basis of many European legal systems. The essential difference between this doctrine and the rule of law is that *Rechsstaat* requires that the powers of the state be limited by an obligation to act consistently

---

[52] Bingham (2007, p. 69).

[53] See for example Woolf (1995), Laws (1995), Allan (1997), Thomas (2000) and Lakin (2008).

with human dignity.[54] This means that it is not enough that the state obey the law. The validity of the law the state makes be open to challenge on the ground that its content infringes human rights. Because the *Rechsstaat* principle mandates respect for human dignity to an extent that the rule of law does not, it obviously provides a better foundation for civics education.

Once the theoretical underpinning of constitutionalism has been addressed, the rest of civics education should ideally include coverage of the historical events that led to the adoption of a country's constitution; the political forces that affected its content; identification of the institutions of government, their powers and how they interact with each other; how freedoms are protected and the role of the citizen as political actor, both formally as a voter and informally through other means of participation. There is a wealth of experiential techniques that can be used in classrooms to enliven student interest in political participation, including debates, mock elections, classroom parliaments, build-your-own budget exercises, issues analysis and visits to government institutions.[55]

3.3.3 Time Allocation in the Curriculum

Evidence shows that in many countries insufficient time is devoted to civics education. In England, civics is allocated a separate subject within the curriculum, albeit only during Years 7–11 (ages 11–16).[56] However, the civics content is, as a matter of practice, often taught as part of a broader subject called personal, social and health education (PSHE) rather than as a free-standing subject.[57] The picture is also complicated by the fact that there are a variety of funding models for public schools in England, and that 75% of secondary schools are 'academy schools' which are not required to follow the national curriculum, which means that coverage of civics in England is not as uniform as might first appear.[58]

In Australia, the Australian Curriculum provides a syllabus for civics and citizenship education from Years 3–10 (ages 9–16), but the fact that education falls under the control of the States and Territories means that use of the Curriculum is not mandatory, with the result that the extent to which civics and citizenship are taught differs between jurisdictions.[59] Where the Australian Curriculum is used, civics and citizenship are taught as part of Humanities and Social Sciences from Years 3–6 and as a separate subject from Years 7–10.[60] The extent to which civics, whether using the Australian Curriculum or not, is indicated by the fact that the national average

54 Basson and Viljoen (1988, pp. 219–24), von der Pfordten (2024, p. 28).

55 Bennion and Laughlin (2018, p. 290).

56 Department of Education (2014a, p. 6).

57 Jerome et al. (2022, p. 9).

58 Jerome et al. (2022, p. 9).

59 Print (2017, pp. 19–20), Commonwealth of Australia (2025, pp. 5–6).

60 Commonwealth of Australia (2025, pp. 3–4).

time allocation is only 32 min per week.[61] A 2025 survey of teachers found that civics was offered at only 72% of schools,[62] but in only 30% of schools as a separate subject.[63]

Education is also a state matter in the United States, with wide variations between states.[64] Only some states requiring testing of civics up to the end of secondary school: Of the 50 states, 10 impose no civics requirement for high school graduation, 24 require the taking of a civics course and an examination, 14 require a civics course but no examination, while two do not require a civics course but do require an assessment.[65]

The time allocated to civics in France is generous. *Enseignement Moral et Civique* is taught in every year of school, with an allocation of 30 min per week in primary school and two hours per month in secondary school.[66] In addition to this, the mandatory philosophy subject in the final year of school is taught for two hours per week to science and technology students and four hours per week to humanities students.[67]

Civics and citizenship education competes with the many other areas of knowledge that have claims over space in the curriculum. In addition, in many countries education systems are structured on the basis that while a common core of subjects is taught for a certain number of years at secondary school, what students learn during their final two years is determined by the students themselves with no mandatory subjects (apart, perhaps, from the national language). This is understandable, as at this stage of their secondary education students need the flexibility to choose subjects that will best lay a foundation for what they want to study at a tertiary institution. Yet civics arguably has a special claim to mandatory inclusion up to the end of secondary education, not only because of its importance to how a society is governed but also because it is precisely during the final two years of school that young people find themselves on the brink of formal participation in the political system as voters and are most in need of understanding their role as citizens.[68]

There is recognition in some countries that greater consistency and more time is needed for the teaching of civics and citizenship. A 2025 report by the Australian Parliament's Joint Standing Committee on Electoral Matters recommended that the next version of the Australian Curriculum contain a mandatory stand-alone civics and citizenship subject, which would end the variations in coverage between states.[69] However the minimum amount of time that the committee recommended be allocated to it in Years 9 and 10 (which are currently the final two years covered by the

61 Commonwealth of Australia (2025, p. 5).

62 Commonwealth of Australia (2025, p. 131).

63 Commonwealth of Australia (2025, p. 131).

64 Journell (2015).

65 Craitu and Ngalande (2024, p. 2).

66 Graveleau (2015).

67 Lilley (2024).

68 Commonwealth of Australia (2025, pp. 220–21).

69 Commonwealth of Australia (2025, p. 40).

curriculum) was a derisory 10 h *per year*.[70] The committee also recommended that a curriculum for Years 11 and 12 (the final two years of school) be developed and that pilot programmes be delivered in anticipation of these levels being added to the national curriculum.[71] The recommendations of the report have yet to be implemented nationwide, but some states have initiated their own changes. In 2024 the South Australian government announced a new civics education policy in terms of which the time allocated to civics would be increased by requiring Year 7 and 8 students to study civics for an hour per week and integrating civics into all subjects in Year 9 and 10.[72] However it is questionable whether adequate focus will be given to civics if it is taught as part of other subjects rather than being a free-standing subject of its own, and the policy did nothing to address the absence of mandatory civics education in Years 11 and 12. Similarly while the new curriculum announced in New South Wales in 2024 for implementation by 2027 included an increase in the time allocated to civics, it did not include a stand-alone civics subject nor did it extend civics to Years 11 and 12,[73] failures that attracted criticism in a report by the NSW parliament's Joint Standing Committee on electoral matters which recommended the inclusion of a dedicated mandatory civics subject throughout the curriculum.[74]

3.4 The Effect of Civics and Citizenship Education on Constitutional Knowledge and Openness to Constitutional Reform

Assuming that the education system provided students with both the capacity to make value-based judgements and knowledge of the interaction between institutions of government, how effective would this be in producing capable citizens? The difficulty in answering this question lies in identifying an education system where the civics education system had manifested specific discernible shortcomings which were remedied by means of content revision, and where voters' levels of knowledge were surveyed both before and after that revision took place. The alternative to this is to mimic the effect of such a process by posing questions on constitutional matters to voters who lacked the relevant knowledge, presenting them with knowledge that they would be taught under a revised civics education system, and then finally asking the same questions again to see to what extent their responses had changed in light of more comprehensive knowledge.

[70] Commonwealth of Australia (2025, p. 41).

[71] Commonwealth of Australia (2025, p. 42).

[72] Holmes (2024).

[73] Henebery (2024).

[74] Joint Standing Committee on Electoral Matters (2025, pp. 1–2).

Such a survey, focussing on two possible constitutional reforms—a change in the electoral system and becoming a republic—was conducted in Australia in 2025.[75] In the case of each reform, respondents were first asked whether they were in favour of the reform without being provided any background information about it. The same question was then repeated, on this occasion accompanied by detailed information on the effect of the proposed reform.

The first set of questions related to the electoral system. As will be discussed in Chap. 4, the electoral system for the House of Representatives (the lower house, where the government is formed) produces highly disproportionate results because it is based on single-member electorates. The following answers were obtained:

> Under our current electoral system, when elections are held for the Commonwealth Parliament, do parties get seats in proportion to their percentage share of the national first preference vote?

Yes	28%
No	32%
Don't know	40%

The fact that a majority of voters either erroneously thought that seats were allocated in proportion to votes won or did not know whether that was the case, points to widespread lack of awareness about a basic feature of the democratic system.

The next question focussed on the particular objective of fairness of representation:

> Do you think that the electoral system should ensure that parties are allocated seats in Parliament in proportion to their percentage share of the votes they receive throughout Australia?

Yes	73%
No	27%

The next question confronted respondents directly with the difference between an electoral system based on single-member electorates and one based on proportional representation in so far as they affected fairness in representation and the politics of government formation:

> Under the current electoral system for the House of Representatives, MPs are elected in single-member electorates. A single party usually gets enough seats to form government, but parties do not get representation in proportion to their support nationwide. This can even lead to a government coming to power with fewer votes nationwide than were received by the opposition. By contrast, under a proportional representation system, parties always get seats in proportion to their share of the national vote. Governments are usually formed by a coalition of parties which, in combination, will always represent a majority of voters. In light of the above, which of these systems do you prefer:

The current electoral system	49%
Proportional representation	51%

75 The survey results are on file with the author.

The final question relating to the electoral system provided further information on the issue of whether the need for coalitions leads to frequent changes in government—in other words, increases governmental instability, a charge frequently made by opponents of proportional representation:

> While proportional representation systems provide fairer representation than does the single-member electorate system that is currently used for the House of Representatives, some people are concerned that the fact that they almost always lead to coalition governments causes political instability. However, since the end of World War II, there have been the same number of general elections held in the United Kingdom which, like Australia, uses a single-member electoral system, as in Germany, which uses proportional representation. In light of this data, which of the systems do you prefer:
>
> The single-member electoral system 41%
> Proportional representation 59%

The answer to this question is significant because providing facts refuting the argument that proportional representation leads to political instability led to a significant increase in the majority willing to adopt such a system.

The second reform covered by the survey was that of whether Australia should become a republic, an issue which has been debated for decades. The first question provided respondents with information about the way in which the Governor-General exercises their powers is governed by convention rather than law.

> The Governor-General represents the Queen in Australia and is appointed and dismissed by the Queen acting on the advice of the Prime Minister of the day. The Governor General's powers are stated very broadly in the Constitution, and most are left to informal rules, called 'conventions.' These rules are not enforceable by the courts - they rely on the political consequences which would occur if they were breached. Do you think that these powers, and the conditions under which they are exercised, should be expressly included as legally enforceable rules in the Constitution?
>
> Yes 67%
> No 33%

The answer to this question indicated an overwhelming preference for codification of the conventions. The next question asked respondents if they wanted Australia to become a republic. The answer revealed an almost equal division of opinion, which is in line with data provided in other surveys over the past decade[76]:

> Do you think Australia should become a republic - that is, with a President, - appointed or elected by Australians - exercising the powers which are currently exercised by the Governor-General on behalf of the Queen?
>
> Yes 47%
> No 53%

The next question asked respondents which method of choosing a president they would prefer if Australia were to become a republic. Again, these answers correlated with those obtained in previous surveys:

[76] Australian National University (2016), YouGov (2024).

If Australia was to become a republic, which of these methods should be used to choose the President:

Election by the voters	76%
Appointment by the Prime Minister	8%
Election by Parliament	16%

Australia held a referendum in 1999 on a proposal that the country should become a republic with a president chosen by parliament. This model decided upon by a Constitutional Convention whose members were selected in accordance with a mechanism devised by the then government, whose leader was a staunch monarchist. The pro-republic campaign failed to overcome the argument that an elected president might be tempted to breach the conventions governing the discharge of the role—even though that risk also existed in relation to a Governor-General. The referendum proposal was defeated by a wide margin because most republicans wanted a president to be elected and so voted against the proposal put before them. The next question in the survey was designed to ascertain to what extent voters would manifest concern in relation to the argument about the conventions, given the effect it had had on the model of a republic that had been chosen in 1999.

Some people are concerned that if the voters directly elected a President, the President might be tempted to use the fact that they were elected by the people to use the powers of the office contrary to the non-legal rules (conventions) which apply to the office. Is that a concern for you?

Yes	60%
No	40%

The final question asked respondents if their concerns would be met if the powers of the office were codified.

If you are concerned that a directly elected President might use his or her powers contrary to convention, would your concerns be met if these conventions were changed into legally-enforceable provisions in the Constitution?

Yes	71%
No	29%

The significance of this large majority is two-fold. First, in comparison to when the question was asked in the abstract earlier in the survey, support for codification increased after its relevance to a republic had been made apparent in subsequent questions. Second, the fact that codification would decisively address voter concerns in relation to the powers of an elected president shows that a republican model that coupled direct election with codification would have a substantial chance of success at a referendum and, more importantly, showed that apprehension surrounding direct election of a president could be overcome if voters were provided with relevant background information.

The survey results show the obvious positive effect that education has on voter understanding of constitutional issues. It also shows how education can change voter attitudes to constitutional reform. But the results also teach a lesson about civics education and its inter-relationship with the politics surrounding constitutional debate. In Australia the Liberal-National and Labor parties, enjoy a political duopoly. This is the inevitable result of an electoral system based on single-member electorates. It is therefore unsurprising that politicians from these parties vehemently oppose electoral reform. The argument they most often advance is that proportional representation leads to governmental instability.[77] Yet, as indicated in the information accompanying one of the survey questions, data from the United Kingdom and Germany show that that criticism lacks foundation.[78]

Similarly, monarchists who argued against presenting to voters a republic with a directly elected president did so on the basis that the conventional powers of the office would be abused and, more significantly, that it would be impossible to codify the conventions. This was despite numerous examples from Commonwealth countries where codification had taken place.[79] Had accurate information refuting that argument been provided, the likelihood would have been increased that the direct-election model would have been put to voters and that it would have met with success.

The survey points to the deficiencies in civics education, because it was clear that the level of knowledge that respondents brought to the survey was such that they lacked awareness of background knowledge needed to evaluate proposed reforms.

The history of attempts at constitutional reform—in particular that of the republic referendum—shows that politicians exploit voters' lack of knowledge and use disinformation to further their political interests, knowing that most voters lack the capacity to engage in analysis. Politicians thus have an interest in keeping voters uninformed, malleable and likely uncritically to accept what they are told. In other words, politicians have a motive for ensuring that voters do *not* become capable citizens. The most recent example of this arose from referendum held in 2023 on whether the constitution should be amended to establish an advisory body chosen by Indigenous peoples to advise the government on matters affecting them. Opponents of the proposal falsely claimed that the government would be bound to follow such advice, despite the fact that there being nothing in the text, or implied by it, that could lead to that conclusion.[80] This illustrates the stark contrast between politicians' public averments that a well-informed citizenry is the foundation of democracy and their actual conduct, which is directed to exploiting voter ignorance.

Despite this, little has been done to counter disinformation. The Joint Committee on Electoral Matters addressed the problem of misinformation and disinformation in

---

[77] BBC News (2017).

[78] There have been the same number of elections in Germany since 1949 as in the United Kingdom (21 in each country) but German politics has been far more stable, with 11 governments during that period compared to 19 in the United Kingdom.

[79] See, for example, the *Constitution of Barbados* 1966, Arts 61, 65, and 66; the *Constitution of Bahamas* 1973, Arts 73, 74 and 66; the *Constitution of Grenada* 1973, Arts 52 and 58; the *Constitution of Jamaica* 1962, Arts 64, 70 and 71; the *Constitution of Dominica* 1978, Arts 59, 60 and 63; the *Constitution of Malta* 1964, Arts 76. 79, 80 and 81 and the *Constitution of Mauritius* 1968, Arts 57, 59 and 60.

[80] Gilbert + Tobin Centre for Public Law (2023. pp. 50, 70–1).

its 2025 report on civics education, noting that social media platforms can be used to rapidly spread such material to voters and that voters often lack the cognitive skills to determine the veracity of what they have been told. It also noted that voters are particularly vulnerable to material that reinforces their pre-existing beliefs and to material which is couched in emotional terms and which is constantly repeated.[81] While the committee recommended that the Australian Electoral Commission be resourced to develop 'factual, translated resources to counteract disinformation'[82] this was only in the context of its discussion of the difficulties faced by culturally and linguistically diverse people for whom English might not be a first language. There was no recommendation that such a service should be established for the general population. This is an issue that must be addressed if voters are to become capable citizens. The conduct of politicians in undermining good citizenship is discussed in Chap. 6.

References

Allan T (1997) Parliamentary sovereignty: law, politics and revolution. Law Q Rev 113:443–52

Australian Curriculum, Assessment and Reporting Authority (2012) Shape of the Australian curriculum: civics and citizenship paper. http://docs.acara.edu.au/resources/Shape_of_the_Australian_Curriculum__Civics_and_Citizenship_251012.pdf. Accessed 28 March 2025

Australian Curriculum, Assessment and Reporting Authority (2019) Ethical understanding. https://www.australiancurriculum.edu.au/f-10-curriculum/general-capabilities/ethical-understanding/. Accessed 28 March 2025

Australian Curriculum, Assessment and Reporting Authority (2025) National Assessment Programme – Civics and Citizenship 2024 Public Report. Australian Curriculum, Assessment and Reporting Authority, Sydney

Australian National University (2016) Trends in Australian political opinion - results from the Australian election study, 1987–2016. https://australianelectionstudy.org/publications/. Accessed 1 April 2025

Basson D, Viljoen H (1988) South African constitutional law. Juta, Kenwyn

Bennion E, Laughlin X (2018) Best practice in civic education: lessons from the Journal of Political Science Education. J Political Sci Educ 14:287–330

BBC News (2017) Opposing voting reform 'selfish' and 'immoral'. BBC News. Accessed 31 Oct 2017

Bellamy R (2010) Introduction. In: Bellamy R, Palumbo A (eds) (2010) Citizenship. Ashgate Publishing, Farnham

Bingham T (2007) The rule of law. Cambridge Law J 66:67–85

Bufacchi V (2023) Why Cicero matters. Bloomsbury, London

Callan E (1997) Creating citizens: political education and liberal democracy. Clarendon Press, Oxford

Chen (2011) Why is Finland tops in civics? Kennedy B (trans) (2010) Commonwealth Magazine (online), 486. Accessed 8 Dec 2011

Cohen B (1969) The problem with bias. In: Heater D (ed) The teaching of politics. Methuen, London, pp 164–180

[81] Commonwealth of Australia (2025, pp. 73–4).

[82] Commonwealth of Australia (2025, pp. 95–6).

Commonwealth of Australia (2025) Joint standing committee on electoral matters - from classroom to community: civics education and political participation in Australia. Commonwealth of Australia, Canberra

Craitu S, Ngalande J (2024) State civics requirements in 2024. Hoover Institution, Stanford

de Tocqueville (1835) Mayer J and Lerner M (eds) (1968) Democracy in America. Collins, London

Department of Education (2014a) The national curriculum England – key stages 3 and 4 framework document. Department of Education, Manchester

Department of Education (2014b) Promoting fundamental British values as part of SMSC in schools. Department of Education, Manchester

Donadio R (2021) What forces hold a liberal democracy together? What forces can tear a liberal democracy apart? The Atlantic, pp 72–8. Accessed December 2021

Gilbert + Tobin Centre for Public Law (2023) Expert analysis of the 'Official Yes/No Cases' published by the Australian Electoral Commission Constitution Alteration (Aboriginal and Torres Strait Islander Voice) 2023. Sydney. Accessed 28 Aug 2023

Graveleau S (2015). En quoi consiste le nouvel «enseignement moral et civique» mis en place cette rentrée? Le Monde. Accessed 29 Aug 2015

Harris B (2024) The sports grants scandal: constitutional protection of socioeconomic rights as a remedy for Porkbarrelling. James Cook Univ Law Rev 29:43–70

Heater D (1999) What is citizenship? Polity Press, Cambridge

Henderson D (2017) Current practice and future challenges in teaching civics and citizenship. In: Peterson A, Tudball L (eds) Civics and citizenship education in Australia. Bloomsbury, London

Henebery B (2024) Experts respond to NSW Curriculum overhaul. The Educator. Accessed 17 Sept 2024

Hoggan-Kloubert T (2023) Civic Education and indoctrination: overlapping areas and demarcation criteria. In: Hoggan-Kloubert T, Mabrey P, Hoggan C (eds) Transformative civic education in democratic societies. Michigan State University Press, East Lansing, pp 29–41

Holmes D (2024) South Australia overhauls civics education. The Mandarin. Accessed 21 Aug 2024

Humphreys J (2013) Philosophy in schools: how other countries do it. The Irish Times. Accessed 19 Nov 2013

International Association for the Advancement of Educational Achievement (2022) Education for Citizenship in times of global challenge - IEA international civic and citizenship education study 2022 international report. International Association for the Advancement of Educational Achievement, Amsterdam

Jerome L, Sant E, Britton A, Emerson L, James S, Milliken M (2022) Citizenship education in the United Kingdom: comparing England, Northern Ireland, Scotland and Wales. J Soc Sci Educ 21:1–22

Johnson L, Morris P (2012) Critical citizenship education on England and France: a comparative analysis. Comparative Educ 48:283–301

Joint Standing Committee on Electoral Matters (2025) Proposals to increase voter engagement, participation and confidence. New South Wales Parliament, Sydney

Journell W (2015) We still need you! An update on the status of k-12 civics education in the United States. The Teacher 48:630–4

Karvelas P (2018) Lucy Gichuhi threatens to name Liberal insiders who she says bullied colleagues during leadership spill. ABC News. Accessed 4 Sept 2018

Lakin S (2008) Debunking the idea of parliamentary sovereignty: the controlling factor of legality in the British constitution. Oxford J Legal Stud 28:709–34

Laws J (1995) Law and democracy. Public Law 72–93

Lazere D (2011) A core curriculum for civic literacy? In: De Vitis J (ed) Critical civic literacy – a reader. Peter Lang, New York, pp 207–16

Le Roux G (2011) Are French students taught to be more philosophical? France 24. Accessed 16 June 2011

Lickona T (2004) Character matters – how to help our children develop good judgment. Integrity and Other Essential Virtues. Simon & Schuster, New York
Lilley Z (2024) French 2024 Bac exams begin and why philosophy is always first. The Connexion. Accessed 18 June 2024
Lu Y (2024) The compatibility of character education and citizenship education in Aristotelian approaches to moral development. J Moral Educ 1–15
Mansfield G (2023) Building citizens: why philosophy is compulsory in French schools. The Local. Accessed 12 June 2023
Mason A (2007) Public Justifiability, Deliberation and Civic Virtue. Social Theory and Practice 33:679–700
Miller N (2015) More than one third of Australians have not heard of the constitution, survey finds. Sydney Morning Herald. Accessed 21 Feb 2015
National Assessment of Educational Progress (2022) NAEP report card: 2022 NAEP civics assessment. https://www.nationsreportcard.gov/civics/results/achievement/. Accessed 10 April 2025
Oldfield A (1990) Citizenship and community: civic republicanism in the modern world. Routledge, London
Peterson A (2011) Civic republicanism and civic education: the education of citizen. Palgrave Macmillan UK, Houndmills
Plato. The Laws. Cornford F (1970) (trans) Clarendon Press, Oxford
Pring R (2001) Citizenship and schools. In: Crick B (ed) Citizens: towards a citizenship culture. Blackwell Publishers, Oxford, pp 81–9
Print M (2017) The recent history of teaching civics and citizenship education in Australia. In: Peterson A, Tudball L (eds) Civics and citizenship education in Australia. Bloomsbury, London, pp 1989–2015
Rachwani M (2023) 'I don't know what it's about': not enough done to explain the voice referendum, people in western Sydney say. The Guardian. Accessed 5 Oct 2023
Samuelsson M (2016) Education for deliberative democracy: a typology of classroom discussions. Democracy Educ 1:1–9
Schuller T (2001) The need for lifelong learning. In: Crick B (ed) Citizens: towards a citizenship culture. Blackwell Publishers, Oxford, pp 90–9
Smith K, Ksenija N, Perkinson R, Hunter T (2021) Practising democracy from childhood: democratic praxis in Te Ao Māori. Democratic Theory 8:19–38
Stedman L (2011) In the name of democracy – educational policy and civics achievement in the standards era. In: De Vitis J (ed) Critical civic literacy – a reader. Peter Lang, New York, pp 43–62
Thomas E (2000) The relationship of parliament and the courts: a tentative thought or two for the new millennium. Victoria Univ Wellington Law Rev 31:5–36
Teitelbaum K (2011) Critical civic literacy in schools – adolescents seeking to understand and improve the(ir) world. In: De Vitis J (ed) Critical civic literacy – a reader. Peter Lang, New York, pp 11–26
United Nations (2010) Human rights education and the national curriculum - Melbourne declaration on educational goals for young Australians. https://www.ohchr.org/sites/default/files/Documents/issues/education/training/replies/AUSTRALIA_30March2010.pdf. Accessed 8 April 2025
von der Pfordten D (2024) On the foundations of the rule of law and the principle of the legal state/ Rechtsstaat. In: Silkenat JR, Hickey JE, Barenboim P (eds) The legal doctrines of the rule of law and the legal state (Rechtstaat). Springer, Cham, pp 14–28

Whiteley P (2012) Political participation in Britain – the decline and revival of civic culture. Palgrave Macmillan, Basingstoke

Woolf H (1995) Droit public – English style. Public Law 57–71

YouGov (2024) 25 years after the referendum: support for a republic declines. YouGov, 7 November 2024. https://au.yougov.com/politics/articles/50879-25-years-after-the-referendum-support-for-a-republic-declines. Accessed 1 April 2025

Zyngier D (2012) Monash University press release. Monash University. https://www.monash.edu/news/opinions/teaching-for-democracy-not-just-about-it-how-should-we-teach-civics. Accessed 28 March 2025

Chapter 4
Constitutional Rights and Their Effect on Citizenship

Abstract Even assuming an effective system of civics and citizenship education, whether people are able to exercise their role as citizens depends upon the extent to which a country's constitution protects human rights. This chapter starts by discussing human rights theory, the way in which a bill of rights ensures protection of human rights and how the concept of proportionality is used to determine whether limitations of rights are justified. The chapter then addresses the argument that a bill of rights undermines democracy, arguing that that argument is based on a misconception of what democracy is and also fails to recognise that unrestrained democracy is inconsistent with human dignity. The remainder of the chapter discusses the right to vote, which is of specific relevance to citizenship in that for many citizens, casting a vote is the only occasion on which they participate in political processes. In the context of voting, the principle of citizen equality requires not only that each adult has a vote but that each vote is of equal effect, and this in turn depends on a country's electoral system. The chapter compares four of the most commonly used electoral systems and determines the extent to which they satisfy the criterion of vote effectiveness and yield results that accurately reflect voter sentiment. The chapter concludes with a discussion of the effect of electoral systems on broader citizen participation in politics.

4.1 Constitutional Rights and their Effect on Citizenship

Preceding chapters of this book discussed the concept of good citizenship, the practices through which effect can be given to good citizenship and how a civics and citizenship curriculum should be designed. But no matter how committed citizens are to good values and no matter how well-informed about constitutional processes, the extent to which they are either willing or able to give effect to good citizenship depends on constitutional structures. No degree of theoretical commitment to good citizenship will suffice if the way these structures operate hinders citizens in their practice of citizenship. The way a constitution is structured either promotes or inhibits the flourishing of good citizenship. This chapter examines two important

B. Harris, *Cultivating Good Citizenship*,
SpringerBriefs in Law, https://doi.org/10.1007/978-981-92-2740-2_4

issues which determine whether good citizenship can flourish: the extent to which human rights in general are protected and how to ensure that the right to vote is effective.

4.2 Human Rights Protection

Self-evidently, a person's capacity to function as a citizen depends on the protection of legal rights. Engagement in reasoned debate requires protection for freedom of thought and speech, while broader forms of participation require protection for freedom of movement and association. But these are just specific examples of the application of a more general principle. As discussed in Chap. 1, human dignity requires respect for individual autonomy or, as Rawls framed it, respect for each individual's liberty to the extent compatible with the equal entitlement to liberty of everyone else. To achieve this, the legal system must protect the individual and communal rights that are needed for people to act with autonomy.

A right is of no value unless the law provides a remedy in cases of infringement. This is true of any legal right but has special implications when it comes to rights protecting individual freedoms. This is because effective protection of these rights requires that a restraint be placed on the organs of the state. Without a mechanism to control the power of the legislature which makes law and the executive which enforces it, rights are vulnerable to abrogation or elimination. Such rights as are protected by the common law or which might be listed in an ordinary statute lack such security, because they can be repealed at the will of the legislature, just like any other law. The very concept of 'human rights' is meaningless unless rights are shielded from legislative over-ride, because the essence of human rights is that they are implied by human dignity, which is inalienable.

A law protecting human rights must itself be protected against amendment or repeal by the legislature. Since the most important function of a bill of rights is to prevent the legislature from enacting laws that infringe human rights, that function would be compromised if the legislature had the power to circumvent the bill of rights. In the absence of some protective procedural mechanism, the legislature could remove the protection provided by a bill of rights by enacting a statute that repealed or amended it. Under the doctrine of implied repeal, which states that a later law impliedly repeals earlier legislation that is inconsistent with it, a legislature could easily nullify the protection offered by a bill of rights even without expressly stating that it was doing so, because the later law would over-ride the bill of rights to the extent that the two laws were inconsistent. Such a bill of rights would not be worth the paper it was written on. The way to protect a bill of rights is to use the device of entrenchment. This would require that the law protecting human rights not be able to be amended or repealed by a simple legislative majority and would stipulate a special procedure that needed to be complied with. In most jurisdictions this is achieved by incorporating the bill of rights into a constitution that is itself entrenched. The entrenchment procedure might consist of a requirement that an amendment be passed by a special majority of the legislature. In most instances a two-thirds or three-quarters majority is required so as to make it unlikely that a government could amend the bill of rights on its own. Alternatively, or in addition to a special legislative majority, the bill of rights might be protected by the requirement that it be approved by voters in a referendum—again with something greater than a simple majority being required. In some countries, parts of the bill of rights are absolutely entrenched—that is, are unamendable. Examples of this are provided by the Namibian constitution, which provides that the bill of rights cannot be amended,[1] and the German constitution which prohibits amendment of the rights to human dignity and to resist unconstitutional action.[2]

The other requirement for effective protection of rights is that the bill of rights be justiciable – that is, enforceable by the courts. A bill of rights that is not enforceable is worthless. A person whose rights have infringed must have the right to approach courts which have the power to enforce the bill of rights by granting an appropriate remedy. This might be a declaration that a statute passed by the legislature or a decision by a member of the executive is invalid. It might include the granting of an injunction either prohibiting or mandating conduct on the part of a person or agency that has breached the bill of rights or is about to do so. It could also include awarding damages to a person whose rights have been infringed.

There are numerous examples of comprehensive bills of rights modelled on the international human rights documents adopted in the wake of World War II—the 1948 *Universal Declaration of Human Rights*, the 1966 *International Covenant on Civil and Political Rights* (ICCPR) and the 1966 *International Covenant on Economic, Social and Cultural Rights* (ICESCR). These foundational documents were drafted in order to protect the inherent equality and dignity of the individual and his or her entitlement to self-realisation. They were adopted by the international community in the wake of the post-World War II war crimes trials in which international tribunals rejected the defence that obedience to the law excused acts contrary to fundamental principles of humanity.[3] The same approach was adopted by post-war German courts, which invalidated Nazi laws authorising breaches of fundamental rights.[4] These courts operated on the basis that human dignity sets limits on the law-making capacity of the state and that state sovereignty was subordinate to supra-legal values. The same philosophy is embodied in the international covenants—the rights they guarantee are universal and are superior to the law of particular states. Of course it is true that, as an observable fact, different societies have different values which are reflected in law which may be inconsistent with the values embodied in the covenants. But the lesson of Nuremberg is that the mere fact of the existence of such values or the law made in accordance with them does not mean that they are as equally valid as the covenants. The rights the covenants protect are founded upon the objective entitlement of people

[1] Namibian Constitution 1990 Arts. 131 and 132(5)(a).

[2] Basic Law for the Federal Republic of Germany 1949, Arts. 1, 20 and 79(3).

[3] For a comprehensive discussion of the Nuremberg Trials see Office of the United States Chief Counsel for the Prosecution of Axis Criminality (1946).

[4] Fuller (1957–58), Mertens (2003).

to human dignity, which is universal and applies to all people at all times and cannot be denied by any national law. In order to give the broadest possible protection to rights, the covenants were drafted in such a way as to express rights in as general a manner as possible, covering core aspects of the human condition or, to adopt a Rawlsian perspective, specifying the full range of rights which a rational person would want to have protected. Among the bills of rights that are closely modelled on the international covenants are those contained in the constitutions of Germany, Canada and South Africa.

4.2.1 Limitation of Rights

There is no such thing as an absolute right, nor are rights hierarchical—each is important. Yet rights may need to be limited in order to serve a social interest. A right may also need to be limited when it comes into conflict with another right. Resolution of these issues requires that some mechanism be included in the bill of rights that the courts can use to determine whether a limitation on a right is justified or, in cases where rights conflict, which should limit the other. There are a variety of tests used in different jurisdictions for this purpose, but two which are broadly similar, and which impose a strict standard for derogation from rights, are those from Canada and South Africa.

In Canada the test formulated by the Supreme Court in *R v Oakes*[5] provides that a law limiting a right contained in the Canadian Charter of Rights and Freedoms will be constitutional only if the following are satisfied:

1. The law must serve a pressing and substantial objective.
2. The law must be proportional, which requires that
   (i) the law must be rationally connected to the objective
   (ii) the law must impair rights to the minimal extent possible and
   (iii) there must be proportionality between the impairment of rights and the objective served by the law.

In South Africa, s 36 of the Constitution states:

36. **Limitation of rights**
(1) The rights in the Bill of Rights may be limited only in terms of law of general application to the extent that the limitation is reasonable and justifiable in an open and democratic society based on human dignity, equality and freedom, taking into account all relevant factors, including

the nature of the right;
the importance of the purpose of the limitation;
the nature and extent of the limitation;

[5] [1986] 1 S.C.R. 103, 138–40.

the relation between the limitation and its purpose; and
less restrictive means to achieve the purpose

(2) Except as provided in subsection (1) or in any other provision of the Constitution, no law may limit any right entrenched in the Bill of Rights.

The test in South Africa imposes a higher standard than the one in Canada in that the courts consider not only the importance of the purpose of the limitation, but also whether (along with the other four factors listed in s 36(1)) a limitation on a right is justifiable in 'an open and democratic society based on human dignity, equality and freedom.'

By balancing individual rights against other social interests, these tests strike a balance between individualism and communitarianism which, as was discussed in Chap. 1, are the complementary strands of citizenship inherent in civic republicanism. They are also consistent with Rawls' liberty principle that each person should enjoy such liberty as is compatible with the equal liberty of others.

4.2.2 Human Rights and Democracy

Notwithstanding the strength of the theoretical argument in favour of a bill of rights, proposals to introduce a constitutional bill of rights in jurisdictions that do not have them have encountered the argument that, by giving the courts the power to invalidate legislation, bills of rights are undemocratic. The typical phraseology is that adopted (among many others) by Australian academic Frank Brennan who argues that a bill of rights would give ultimate power over the law to 'unelected judges.'[6] Even in countries which have bills of rights, the courts have been attacked on grounds of alleged obstruction of the popular will—multiple examples of this being provided by statements by US President, Donald Trump.[7]

At the heart of the question of whether the democratic will should be restrained by a bill of rights lies the conflict between Nietzchean and dignitarian philosophy. As discussed in Chap. 1, Nietzchean theory holds that human relationships should be determined solely on the basis of power and that restraints on power lead to a weakening of society. By contrast, dignitarian theory views each person as entitled to equal autonomy and holds that power, even democratic power, cannot be the final arbiter of the extent to which people are entitled to enjoy human dignity. The principle was succinctly stated by James Madison who wrote[8]

> It is of great importance in a republic, not only to guard the society against the oppression of its rulers, but to guard one part of the society against the injustice of the other part.

---

[6] Brennan (2015, p. 271).

[7] Gregory (2025).

[8] Madison (1788, p. 412).

Democracy is a reflection of the aggregate views of voters acting (as they are entitled to do) in their own self-interest. But while self-interested decision making is suitable for pragmatic questions such as what the speed limit should be or at what level a sales tax should be set, it cannot form the basis for deciding qualitatively different decisions that engage values, such as what the rights of people charged with crimes should be or the extent to which freedom of religion should be limited. These are ethical questions where one person's view is not equally valid as another's and must be answered by reference to values external to the preferences of majorities. An example that contrasts the clash between these two types of decision-making is provided by the issue of same-sex marriage which came to prominence in a number of jurisdictions in recent years. In the case of Australia, a plebiscite was held in 2017 on whether same-sex marriage should be legalised. During the course of the campaign, former Prime Minister Tony Abbott said 'And I say to you if you don't like same-sex marriage, vote no,'[9] a statement which reflects a view that whether one segment of the population should be able to make an intimate life choice should depend on the approval of another. By contrast in its decision in *Obergefell v Hodges*[10] the US Supreme Court ruled that prohibitions on same-sex marriage were unconstitutional because they infringed the right to privacy protected by the bill of rights. The court held that the theory underpinning the bill of rights is that freedom to exercise fundamental rights is not contingent on democratic process[11] and that '[a]n individual can invoke a right to constitutional protection when he or she is harmed, even if the broader public disagrees and even if the legislature refuses to act', because 'fundamental rights may not be submitted to a vote; they depend on the outcome of no elections.'[12]

The argument that a bill of rights undermines democracy, or is in conflict with it, is based on a misunderstanding of the nature of both human rights and of democracy. Democracy itself is not a right—it is a *mechanism of government*, just like monarchy, oligarchy or dictatorship. But although democracy is itself not a right, it is the form of government that *results from the granting of a right*—namely the right of people to vote for their lawmakers. This right exists because human dignity requires that each person enjoy political power equal to that of every other person, and the only way to achieve that is by giving each adult person a right to vote for the body that makes laws. In exercising their right to elect law-makers, voters ultimately exercise a power to make law that binds their fellow citizens. So an exercise of the right to vote constitutes both an exercise of each voter's autonomy *and* an imposition of a limit on the autonomy of others through their subjection to the law made on the voter's behalf.

While the statement 'everyone should have a right to vote' is uncontroversial, the question which many, and perhaps most, people have not thought about is *why* people should have that right. What is the source of the right? The right to vote must be able

---

9 Hunter (2017).

10 576 U.S. 644 (2015).

11 576 U.S. 644 (2015) 23–6.

12 576 U.S. 644 (2015) 24.

to be justified by something external to it—it is not something free-standing or self-justifying. The answer is that that right, like all other rights, derives from the ultimate value of respect for human dignity. As we saw in Chap. 1, human dignity requires respect for the equal autonomy of each individual which, in the context of political rights, means the right of each adult person to vote in order to exercise law-making power through their representatives. However, since rights are non-hierarchical, and human dignity requires respect for all rights, the right to vote is not superior to any other right. The right to vote—and more specifically, the legislation that is enacted as a consequences of voters exercising that right—must be balanced against other rights in cases where they conflict. The right of each citizen to exercise political power by voting for a legislature does not trump all the other rights that citizens are entitled to. Liberty is not true liberty if it is limited to only so much liberty as a bare majority of one's fellow citizens are prepared to allow. The fact that a restriction on a freedom derives from the exercise of power by legislators elected by the people does not in itself justify the restriction. Whether the restriction is justified depends on a balancing of the interests served by the legislation against the extent to which the right has been limited, using a proportionality test.

An illustration of what the consequences could be if legislative power was unconstrained is provided by the following argument: During the apartheid era, the South African parliament, whose members were elected solely by the white population comprising 20% of the total, enacted legislation oppressive of the 80% majority. This legislation embodied a system of racial classification, segregating access to public facilities, health and education systems, delineating separate residential areas for different races and prohibiting inter-racial sexual intercourse or marriage. The edifice was supported by legislation restricting civil liberties. The apartheid system was obviously incompatible with human dignity and breached multiple human rights. For that reason it was universally condemned. But, what if the situation in South Africa had been *reversed*, and a parliament for which 80% of the population could vote had enacted the same laws oppressing the remaining 20%? Or, to posit yet another scenario, what if the entire population was enfranchised and a government which had won the support of 51% of voters enacted apartheid-type legislation that discriminated against the other 49%? The answer to these questions is surely that the legislation would still be considered unjust. Support by a majority of voters would not change its oppressive character or its incompatibility with human dignity. Majority support cannot not transform what is evil into what is good. Apartheid legislation was inherently wrong because of its *effect on those oppressed*, which would be the same irrespective of whether they constituted 80% or 49% of the population. It is the *content* of law, not the level of support it enjoys, that determines its effect and whether it is consistent with human dignity. The question of whether a law is 'just' or 'unjust' is meaningless in a society ruled by unrestrained majoritarianism because whether a law is valid depends solely on the balance of public opinion, whereas the concepts of 'just' and 'unjust' imply the existence of a standard of values external to the popular will against which the validity of law can be judged. There is no shortage of examples where the power of a majority has deprived individuals and minorities of their dignity, a recent example of which is provided by the Philippines, where its president, Rodrigo Duterte, retained widespread popularity despite of—and indeed because of—gross violations of the rights of people suspected of drug trafficking.[13]

The reason why bills of rights attract such fervent opposition from politicians is that they provide an effective curb on their power. The argument that peoples' right to control over government is undermined if judges are given the power to strike down legislation on grounds of inconsistency with a bill of rights is a populist distortion. It exploits the fact that people are generally unaware of the theoretical underpinnings of human rights and lack an understanding that democracy is a product of rights rather than rights being a product of democracy. It also represents the consequences of a bill of rights for power relationships. Far from undermining citizen power, a bill of rights *augments* citizen power by giving citizens the ability to challenge the validity of legislation that unduly limits their freedoms. It is the fact that that augmentation comes at the expense of the power wielded by politicians that is the true basis of politicians' opposition to a bill of rights.[14]

Finally, the argument that because they are unelected, judges should not have the power to over-ride legislation misconstrues the difference between the legislative and judicial function. When people cast their vote, they are entitled—indeed expected—to vote in accordance with their own self-interest and to their maximum advantage. They are also entitled to cast their vote without regard to the interests or, importantly, the rights, of others. They are entitled to cast their vote in accordance with any prejudices they have. Politicians are similarly entitled to act out of self-interest in enacting legislation that will redound to their political advantage. But when voters elect politicians who, acting in the name of the voters, enact law limiting the rights of other citizens, some restraint must be in place to ensure that the rights that those other citizens are entitled to by virtue of their dignity are not unduly restricted. As discussed in Chap. 1, a society not founded upon, and subject to, the value of human dignity will be one in which the weak are dominated by the strong. The only way in which legislative power can be restrained and the entitlement to human dignity upheld is by means of a bill of rights applied by independent courts. The judicial function is different. It is precisely *because* judges are unelected that they are able to discharge the role of determining disputes between citizens whose rights have been restricted and the legislature that has restricted them. Unlike voters or politicians, judges do not decide questions in accordance with their personal interest. Judges have no constituency to please and personal gain to be derived from the decisions they make. Their role is to determine disputes impartially and without regard to the political interests of the parties involved. It is in this neutrality that their strength lies—and indeed why politicians would rather not have them scrutinise their exercise of legislative power.

---

[13] Ratcliffe (2022).

[14] Robertson (2009, p. 8).

4.3 The Electoral System

The right to vote is just one of the many rights that needs the protection afforded by a bill of rights. However, it merits particular analysis, because for most citizens, voting is the only occasion on which they participate in political processes.

Like all other rights, the right to vote derives from human dignity, and gives effect to the principle that dignity requires that each person have an equal share in political power. This means that, to conform to the requirements of human dignity, an electoral system must confer equal political power on each citizen, both in form and in fact. There are many countries in which, in a formal sense, citizens have a 'right to vote' in that they are able to go to a polling place and signify a choice on a ballot paper. But these countries are not truly democratic because they do not satisfy the preconditions necessary for the casting of a vote to be of real effect, including the ability of people to form political parties and to stand for election, protection of freedom of expression, freedom to operate independent media, and the conduct of elections in accordance with procedural fairness. So the mere right to cast a vote is not enough—what is also required is that each citizen has equal political power *in fact*—in other words, that the electoral system ensures that each person's vote has the same *impact* as that of every other or, as researchers in the field of electoral systems express it, that each vote is of equal effectiveness.

This means that it is not enough even if the electoral system is one where multiple parties are permitted to contest elections, where there is a free press and where elections are conducted fairly. For example, in several countries during the colonial era, Indigenous voters were put on a separate voters' roll to white voters, and elected MPs to a number of seats that was tiny in comparison to what their proportion of the population would have entitled them. Formally speaking, these voters, like white voters, each had a vote, but the effect of their votes was negligible because of the relationship between votes and seats. To be truly democratic, a system must ensure that every vote must, as far as is practicable, have an equal impact on the composition of the legislature. This is a matter of degree rather than of absolutes. One could arrange electoral systems along a continuum, from least to most democratic, depending on the extent to which they met that criterion. This part of the chapter compares five of the most commonly used electoral systems and determines the extent to which they satisfy the criterion of vote effectiveness and yield results that accurately reflect voter sentiment.

4.3.1 First Past the Post (FPP)

Under First Past the Post (FFP) a country is divided into electoral districts which each return a single member to the legislature.[15] Each voter casts a single vote for the candidate they prefer. The winning candidate needs only obtain a plurality

---

[15] Carter et al. (2024, pp. 11–36).

of votes—that is, more votes than any other candidate. This means that winning candidates frequently obtain fewer than a majority of votes cast. Indeed, a candidate can win with significantly fewer than a majority of votes. To take a hypothetical example, if there were five candidates in an electoral district, four of whom each received 19% of the votes cast, the fifth would win having obtained only 24% of the vote. It is also notable that the votes of the four losing candidates—totalling 76% of votes cast—have no effect on the composition of the legislature, a situation which is obviously incompatible with the principle of equality of voting power. Because of the potential for this type of arbitrary result, voters are forced to vote strategically—that is, instead of voting for the candidate they actually support, they vote for whichever they prefer of the two candidates who are most likely to be elected or, to put it more bluntly, will vote for whichever of those candidates they dislike less.[16] This in turn leads to politics being dominated by two major parties.[17]

On a macro-level, further shortcomings of FPP become evident. As is unavoidable in the case of any system based on geographically-defined electorates, the positioning of boundaries between electoral districts has a dramatic effect on party performance. In other words, the critical factor that determines the outcome of elections is not how much support a party has, but rather the placement of boundaries between electoral districts and the accident of where the party's supporters happen to be located relative to them.

There is general consensus that the most important factor in determining the proportionality of electoral systems is 'district magnitude'—that is, the number of members elected from each geographical electorate.[18] The lower the district magnitude, the less proportional the results. As is discussed in the following sections of this chapter, some electoral systems use multi-member electoral districts, thereby enhancing proportionality. FPP, in having electoral districts that return only one member (in other words, a district magnitude of 1) inevitably produces the least proportionate –or the most disproportionate—results of any electoral system.

The adverse effect that geographic boundaries have on proportionality is also affected by the total number of seats in the assembly, because the fewer the number of seats, the more the disproportionality of the system is magnified.[19] In this context 'smaller' refers both to the absolute number of seats and to the number of seats relative to voting population (or, to express it differently, the number of voters each legislator represents).[20]

Finally a general point of criticism that can be levelled at FPP is that since the system usually results in two main parties having a large number of safe seats, and elections are determined by the results in a few marginal seats, the difference between

[16] Blais and Geschwend (2010, pp. 186–9), Hix et al. (2010, p. 48).
[17] Givens (2025).
[18] Carter et al. (2024, pp. 6, 161–2).
[19] Kjaer and Elklit (2014, pp. 159, 169–71).
[20] Allen and Stoll (2023, pp. 1–2, 10–11).

a party winning a majority of seats can depend on the decisions of a relatively small number of voters.[21]

4.3.2 Alternative Vote (AV)

The AV (Alternative Vote) system shares with FPP the fact that each electoral district returns one member to the legislature which, like FFP, leads to a two-party system. For these reasons it has been viewed as simply a variation of FFP.[22] The difference between the two systems is that under AV a candidate must obtain an absolute majority +1 of votes cast.[23] This is achieved by means of voters indicating a preference between candidates standing in their electoral district. If, after counting the first preference votes, no candidate has obtained a majority, the candidate with the fewest first preference votes is eliminated and their votes are distributed to whoever their voters gave their second preference votes. If, after this distribution of second preferences, there is still no candidate with an absolute majority, the candidate with the lowest number of votes is eliminated and their votes given to the candidate who was the third preference in their ballot papers. The elimination and distribution process continues until a candidate obtains and absolute majority.[24]

Although AV eliminates the possibility that exists under FPP of a candidate with less than a majority (and possibly far less than a majority) of votes being elected, the system still manifests many of the flaws of FPP. The fact that voters have the opportunity to rank candidates and so, technically speaking, votes are not wasted as they all contribute to the accumulation of preferences, this is true only up to the penultimate stage of a count, because votes cast for the losing candidate in the final round have no effect on the composition of the legislature. Also as, is the case with FPP, where the candidate that a voter truly supports has little chance of being elected, the voter is forced to vote tactically and, ultimately, to vote for whichever of the final two candidates they find least odious. Similarly, the fact that the system is based on single member electorates means that the placement of boundaries between electoral districts can have a decisive effect on a party's performance. On a national level, AV leads to dominance by two major blocs and distortions very similar to those resulting from FPP,[25] with elections often being determined by results on a few marginal seats.[26] AV is used in Australia where in recent years, growing disaffection with the two blocs that dominate politics (the Liberal / National Coalition and Labor) has led to an increase in the number of first preference votes cast for other parties. In 2007 14.5% of first preference votes went to the Greens, another minor party or

[21] Hix et al. (2010, pp. 19, 45–6).

[22] Rae (1971, pp. 107–8, 113).

[23] Carter et al. (2024, pp. 46–63).

[24] Hix et al. (2010, p. 51).

[25] Carter et al. (2024, pp. 53, 60)

[26] For an example from Australia, see Harris (2020, pp. 68–9).

an independent. This increased steadily in succeeding elections and reached 25% in 2019 and 34.4% in 2025. Yet this yielded only 13 seats (or 8.6%) in the 150 House of Representatives. In all other seats those voters had ultimately to choose between a Labor or Coalition candidates who could actually win the seat, but with whom those voters had no affinity.

4.3.3 Single Transferrable Vote (STV)

The Single Transferrable Vote (STV) system is used in Ireland, Malta and in elections for the lower houses in Tasmania and the Australian Capital Territory. It is also used elections for the Australian Senate, for various state upper houses. It differs from FPP and AV in that although the country is divided into electoral districts, each district returns multiple representatives to the legislature.[27] This means that parties may nominate as many candidates as there are seats to be filled in a district. Voters indicate an ordered preference between candidates. An important feature of STV is that in contrast to FPP and AV where political parties determine who their candidate will be in each district, under STV there can be as many candidates from the same party as there are seats to fill. The fact that voters can allocate preferences down the entire list of candidates means that they are able to rank candidates from the same party differently and so determine which (if any) of a party's candidates will be elected. This diminishes the power of parties to determine who represents them in the legislature. The system for counting votes is complex: In order to be elected, a candidate must accumulate enough votes to reach the 'quota' for the district, defined as the number of votes cast divided by the number of seats in the electorate plus one seat, plus one vote. If a candidate reaches the quota after counting of first preferences, the number of votes they received in excess of the quota is distributed among other candidates in proportion to how second preferences were allocated by all the elected candidate's voters. If no candidate reaches the quota after that distribution, the candidate with the lowest number of votes at that stage is eliminated, and their third preference votes are transferred to the remaining candidates. The process continues until all seats are filled.

Like the AV system, STV enables each vote to be effective until the last round of distribution (assuming that voters exhaust their votes by indicating a preference among all candidates), consequently only the votes cast for the last remaining candidate(s) have no effect on the composition of the legislature. However, an advantage of STV is that because more than one representative is elected from each district, the distortion of results caused by geographically defined districts is lessened because the existence of multi-member electoral districts means that there are fewer districts, which in turn means fewer boundaries and thus fewer instances where the performance of parties is adversely affected by concentrations of their voters being divided by boundaries.

[27] Carter et al. (2024, pp. 129–56).

The extent to which STV produces results where seats gained by parties is proportionate to the votes they obtained depends on the number of seats to be filled in each electoral district: the greater the number of seats, the more proportionate the results. This is demonstrated by observing the effect of changing the number of representatives per seat as occurred in Tasmania. Between 1959 and 1996, and again from 2024, the legislature consisted of 35 members elected from five electoral districts, each returning seven members. However, the chamber was reduced to 25 between 1998 and 2023, with each electoral district returning five members. Analysis of election results shows a far greater degree of proportionality during the eras when each electorate returned seven members as compared to when they each returned five.[28]

Another indicator of the importance of seats per district is whether a party or coalition has been able to win government with less than an absolute majority of first preference votes. In a truly proportional system that should not be possible. In the eight elections in Tasmania when there were seven seats per district, no governments came to power with a minority of votes, but in the eight when the number of seats per electoral district was reduced to five, three governments came to power with less than a majority of first preference votes.[29]

STV has been criticised on the ground that in some jurisdictions where it has been used, it has resulted in unwieldy ballot papers with dozens of candidates to be ranked by voters.[30] However, this problem can be overcome by allowing voters to choose *either* to indicate preferences among candidates *or* to indicate preferences between parties, in which case their vote is distributed in accordance with preferences lodged by the parties prior to the election. Alternatively, (or in addition) voters may be allowed to vote for a minimum number of individual candidates, rather than being required to indicate preferences among all of them. This is the case on Senate elections in Australia, where voters can either allocate a minimum of six preferences between parties or a minimum of 12 preferences between candidates.[31]

4.3.4 Proportional Representation (PR)

Proportional Representation (PR) systems come in a number of variations. The simplest form is nationwide PR using a closed list. Under this system, which is used in Israel, there are no electoral districts.[32] Before the election each party publishes an ordered list of candidates equal to the number of seats in the legislature. Voters cast their vote for parties rather than candidates, and each party obtains a proportion

[28] Tasmanian Electoral Commission (2025).

[29] In 1989, 2006 and 2021.

[30] Hix et al. (2010, pp. 74–5).

[31] Australian Electoral Commission (2025).

[32] For an example of election results obtained under PR in Israel see Shugart and Taagepera (2017, p. 75).

of legislative seats equal to its percentage of its nationwide vote.[33] This is the most proportional system of representation achievable, because the entire country forms one electoral district, so the district magnitude equals the number of seats in the legislature. The lists are 'closed' in that each party determines the ranking of candidates on its list. This means that voters are unable to affect who among the candidates will fill the seats it wins. The system produces complete proportionality, with every vote contributing to the composition of the legislature and no wasted votes. However, voters have no identifiable local representative to whom they can turn for assistance in their dealings with the government and, as already stated, they also have no control over which of a party's candidates are elected.

The variations of PR depend on the interplay of two factors—whether lists are open or closed and whether elections are conducted using a single nationwide list or from lists in a number of multi-member districts.

Under open list PR, voters are not required to accept the order in which candidates are ranked by parties. Instead a voter casts a vote for a particular candidate. Once the total number of votes received by a party's candidates is tallied, the party is allocated seats in proportion to that share of the vote, after which seats are allocated to its candidates in order of votes received.[34] Although this means that the identity of candidates rests in the hands of voters, the problem of voters not having an identifiable local representative remains if there is a single nationwide list.

The second variation of PR seeks to address the problem of local representation by dividing the country into a number of regions, each returning a number of legislators proportionate to its population. PR elections are conducted from party lists (ether closed or open) within each region. However, this involves a trade-off between proportionality and having identifiable representatives: The more numerous the districts, the smaller the number of representative returned from each and the lesser the degree of proportionality that is achievable. This is the inevitable consequence of reducing district magnitude.[35] On the other hand, the larger the districts and the more numerous the representatives returned from each, the less the degree to which representatives can be seen as local.

Finally, one can combine open lists with multi-member districts, in an attempt both to give voters control over which of a party's candidates on its list are elected and to provide local representation. This is widely used in Europe, including in countries such as Belgium, Denmark, Finland and Austria to name but a few.[36] The combination of open lists with multi-member districts has been shown to lead to voters contacting representatives more frequently than in FPP or closed list PR systems,[37] and representatives have a strong inducement to be responsive to voter requests for assistance.[38] Such a system can ultimately end up being almost the

[33] Carter et al. (2024, pp. 65–92).

[34] Carter et al. (2024, p. 90).

[35] Carter et al. (2024, p. 74).

[36] Hix et al. (2010, p. 61).

[37] Hix et al. (2010, p. 23).

[38] Farrell (2001, p. 171).

same as STV (where voter interaction with their representatives is also high).[39] The difference between the two systems is that under PR, voters choose a candidate from only one party and seats are allocated according to the percentage of votes a party obtains in each district, whereas under STV voters can express preferences across party lines (indeed, between all candidates standing in the district) and seats are allocated by means of vote transfers.

4.3.5 *Mixed Member Proportional (MMP)*

The Mixed Member Proportional (MMP) system is a hybrid of FPP and PR, in which half the legislative seats are filled via single member electoral districts and half from ordered party lists.[40] Each voter has two votes, one to elect a representative from their electoral district, the other to select whichever party they prefer. Once the results from electoral districts are known, the remaining seats are filled from party lists in such a way that the percentage of each seats that each party has in the legislature (electoral district seats plus list seats) is the same as the percentage of list votes it obtained nationwide. As under PR, which of a party's candidates fills its list seats is determined by reference to its ranked list (disregarding candidates who have been successful in obtaining an electoral district seat). The system is thus highly proportional and whereas voters may find it necessary to use their electoral district vote tactically and vote for a party that they do not support in order to avoid the seat being won by a party they prefer less, having a list vote means that they can vote for whichever party they truly support. The ability to cast a lost vote also means that each voter has an impact on the composition of the legislature. In some jurisdictions a minimum requirement is imposed for an entitlement for a share in list seats. In Germany a party must either win at least three electoral district seats or at least 5% of the list vote to have list seats allocated to it. The same applies in New Zealand. While a threshold requirement slightly reduces the degree of proportionality achieved by the system, the results it achieves are still highly reflective of nationwide support for each party.[41]

4.3.6 *Comparative Analysis*

As stated at the start of this chapter, the degree to which an electoral system accurately reflects levels of voter support for political parties is the key determinant of how effective is a person's vote, and also the degree of equality in voting power between citizens. A useful measure of the proportionality of electoral systems accurately is

[39] Hix et al. (2010, p. 23).

[40] Carter et al. (2024, pp. 93–127).

[41] Zeier and Grün (2025).

Country	Electoral system	Gallagher index
Netherlands	PR	1.21
Germany	MMP	2.67
Tasmania 1959-96, 2024[1]	STV	3.46
Tasmania 1998-2021	STV	6.09
Australia (House of Representatives)	AV	9.44
United Kingdom	FPP	11.7

Fig. 4.1 Comparison of electoral systems by levels of disproportionality

Gallagher's Least Squares index, which measures the extent to which shares of the nationwide vote a party gains in an election translates into legislative seats.[42] A low index indicates that an electoral system produces results where the percentage of votes obtained by a party is reflected in the percentage of seats it obtains in the legislature. Conversely, a high index indicates that the percentage of votes obtained does not correspond to the number of seats won. A high index therefore indicates that the electoral system is unfair both to parties which fail to get representation in the legislature proportionate to their support among voters and, obviously, to those voters themselves. An application of the index to the results if elections held in various jurisdictions between 1945 and 2010, each providing an example of one of the electoral systems discussed above, reveals the following (Fig. 4.1).[43]

The high levels of disproportionality produced by FPP and AV means that they obviously fail to secure for voters equal impact on the political process. By contrast, the data unsurprisingly shows the clear superiority of PR in so far as proportionality is concerned. But, as discussed earlier, PR, like any system reliant on party lists, has the defect of not giving voters an identifiable local representative to whom they can take their concerns. In addition, since parties control the order in which candidates appear on their lists, the system denies voters control over the identity of MPs and makes it virtually impossible to vote an unpopular MP out of office if they are placed high enough on a party list.

MMP, open list PR based on multi-member districts and STV all seek to strike a balance between proportionality and identifiable district representation. All produce proportionate results, and therefore satisfy the requirement that each citizen's vote should be of equal impact. However, MMP has the drawback that it allows half the representatives to be elected via lists whose ordering is not subject to control by voters. By contrast, open list PR with multi-member districts, along with STV, give voters control over the choice of representatives, but the proportionality of such a system is highly dependent on the number of representatives allocated to each district.

As between the PR variant and STV, the choice comes down to which is to be preferred between voters having a single vote for one of the candidates of the party they support, or of having the opportunity to rank all candidates in the district. Since the latter system enables voters to influence who is elected in circumstances where their favoured candidate is not, it offers greater choice to voters than does open list

42 Gallagher (1991, pp. 40–1).

43 Shugart and Taagepera (2017, p. 150).

multimember district PR. I would therefore argue that STV, using seven seats per electoral district, strikes a reasonable balance between proportionality and localised representation, while also ensuring maximum effectiveness of each vote. Under such a system the quota in an electoral district would be 12,5% of the vote +1 vote, which would mean that a party would be able to win a seat if it obtained 1/8 of the vote.

An additional consideration that would affect proportionality under STV at national level is the number of seats in the legislature as a whole: the greater the number of seats, both absolutely and on proportion to the number of voters, the greater the number of electoral districts, and the less the distorting effect of electoral boundaries.

4.3.7 The Effect of Electoral Systems on Citizen Participation

There is extensive evidence for the proposition that the type of electoral system affects the level of citizen engagement in political processes.[44] The reason for this is obvious: An electoral system that produces results where there is a disparity between the number of votes a party receives and the number of seats it obtains, creates disillusionment among those whose votes have no impact on the composition of the legislature. Many of these voters will consider it pointless to cast a vote on a system which they believe conclude is stacked against them, which has a depressive effect on turnout. In his analysis of what determines the health of democracy, Whiteley stated as follows:[45]

> …democracy requires its citizens to have a sense of political efficacy, that is, to believe that they can change things if they get involved in the political process. If politics is impervious to the needs of its citizens, either because the key institutions have been captured by unresponsive groups or because individuals are too apathetic to articulate their views, it will wither.

In many countries, certainly those that have electoral systems based on single-member electoral districts, belief on the part of citizens that they can effect change remains a forlorn hope. This is because such electoral systems inevitably lead to capture by unresponsive groups in the form of two major parties. The fact that these parties can be certain that ultimately one or other of them will form government, means that there is little incentive for them to cater to voters falling outside the ranks of their own supporters. It also means that many voters who support a party other than one of the two majors find themselves in the unenviable position of either 'wasting' their vote by casting it in favour of the party they truly support, or of voting for whichever of two dominant parties to support presents the least worse option.[46]

Electoral systems based on single-member electorates produce the greatest level of disparity between votes received and seats won and thus have the greatest negative

---

[44] Karp and Banducci (2008, pp. 312–32).

[45] Whiteley (2012, p. 10).

[46] Singh (2011, p. 647).

effect on voter turnout.[47] By contrast, systems which produce proportionate results are marked by higher levels of turnout,[48] with even higher turnout in systems such as STV where voters can choose between candidates of the same party.[49] Unfair electoral systems also inhibit the formation of new political parties whose potential supporters consider it unlikely that such parties would succeed in obtaining representation.[50] In short, ensuring a fair electoral system is a key element of an institutional environment conducive to good citizenship.

The impact of electoral system design both on citizen rights and on citizen willingness to engage in political processes is obvious, yet is often overlooked, sometimes deliberately so by parties who benefit from systems which advantage them at the expense of equal representation of voters. Paradoxically, despite the fact that it is plainly observable when an electoral system fails to produce proportional results, proponents of reform often have an uphill battle when making their arguments. This is chiefly because systems that are unfair—in particular FPP and AV—typically produce results that give a government a clear (albeit undeserved) majority, which is used as an argument against proportional systems which almost always lead to coalition governments which, it is alleged, are inherently unstable. Yet the data shows not only that that the instability argument is without foundation, but also that voters have a greater degree of satisfaction with politics under proportional systems than they do under systems such as FPP and AV, even if their party lost an election.[51] This may reflect the fact that the two party systems leads to simplistic 'either/or' reasoning and binary decision-making, as compared to multi-polar, multifaced reasoning that leads to consensus-based decision-making in countries where the electoral system produces coalition government—an environment which is far more conducive to citizen engagement.

Finally, a powerful example of the invalidity of the argument that proportional systems produce political instability is provided by the fact that there have been the same number of elections in Germany since 1949 which uses MMP, as in the United Kingdom which uses FPP. The German political system has also been more stable, with 11 Chancellors during that period, in contrast to 18 Prime Ministers in the United Kingdom. The average duration of governments during the period 2002–2020 was 3.8 years in Germany and 2.2 years in the United Kingdom.[52] Quite apart from the principled reasons in favour of adopting a proportional electoral system, the evidence shows that pragmatic arguments against proportional systems are invalid.

---

[47] Whiteley et al. (2010, pp. 33, 37).

[48] Eggers (2015, pp. 156–7).

[49] Hix et al. (2010, p. 16).

[50] Whiteley et al. (2010, pp. 33–6).

[51] Farrell (2001, pp. 204–6).

[52] Clark and Clarke (2025).

References

Allen G, Stoll H (2023) A number most convenient? The representational consequences of legislative size. Electoral Stud 82:1–12

Australian Electoral Commission (2025) How to vote for the Senate. Accessed 2 June 2025

Blais A, Geschwend T (2010) Strategic defection across elections, parties, and voters. In: Dalton R, Anderson C (eds) 2010 Citizens, context and choice: how context shapes citizens' electoral choices. Oxford University Press, Oxford, pp 176–94

Brennan F (2015) No small change: the road to recognition for indigenous Australia. University of Queensland Press, St Lucia

Carter E, Farrell M, Loomes G (2024) Electoral systems: a global perspective, 3rd edn. Bloomsbury Academic, London

Clark A and Clarke S (2025) The rise of the far right, global trade and Ukraine's future: why the German election matters – visual explainer. The Guardian Australia. Accessed 19 Feb 2025

Eggers A (2015) Proportionality and turnout: evidence from French municipalities. Comparative Political Stud 48:135–67

Farrell D (2001) Electoral systems – a comparative introduction. Palgrave, Houndmills

Fuller L (1957–58) Positivism and fidelity to law - a reply to Professor Hart. Harvard Law Rev 71:630–72

Gallagher M (1991) Proportionality, disproportionality and electoral systems. Electoral Stud 10:33–51

Givens T (2025) The impact of strategic voting in Canada. The Conversation, 30 April 2025. https://theconversation.com/the-impact-of-strategic-voting-in-canada-255489. Accessed 6 May 2025

Gregory M (2025) Like many populist leaders, Trump accuses judges of being illegitimate obstacles to safety and democracy. The Conversation. Accessed 23 May 2025

Harris B (2020) Constitutional reform as a remedy for political disaffection in Australia – the discussion we need. Springer, Singapore

Hix S, Johnston R, McLean I, Cummine A (2010) Choosing an electoral system. The British Academy, London

Hunter F (2017) Marriage plebiscite: tony Abbott urges a 'no' vote to reject political correctness and protect religious freedom. The Sydney Morning Herald. Accessed 9 Aug 2017

Karp J, Banducci S (2008) Political efficacy and participation in twenty-seven democracies: how electoral systems shape political behaviour. Br J Political Sci 38:311–34

Kjaer U, Elklit J (2014) The impact of assembly size on representativeness. J Legislative Stud 20:156–73

Madison J (1788) Federalist No. 51. in America's founding documents (2018). Lerner Publishing Group, Minneapolis

Mertens T (2003) Nazism, legal positivism and Radbruch's thesis on statutory injustice. Law and Critique 14(3):277–95

Office of the United States Chief Counsel for the Prosecution of Axis Criminality (1946) Nazi conspiracy and aggression. Government Publications Office, Washington

Rae (1971) The political consequences of electoral laws. Yale University Press, New Haven

Ratcliffe R (2022) 'The Punisher': Rodrigo Duterte's violent reign as Philippines president to end. The Guardian. Accessed 28 June 2022

Robertson G (2009) The statute of liberty: how Australians can take back their rights. Random House Australia, North Sydney

Shugart M, Taagapera R (2017) Votes from seats - logical models of electoral systems. Cambridge University Press, Cambridge

Singh S (2011) Contradictory calculi: differences in individuals' turnout decisions across electoral systems. Political Res Q 64:646–55

Tasmanian Electoral Commission (2025) Election reports. https://www.tec.tas.gov.au/info/Publications/index.html#election_reports. Accessed 13 May 2025

Whiteley et al (2010) Do Institutions Really Influence Political Participation? Contextual influences on turnout and participation in the world's democracies. International Journal of Market Research 52:21–42

Whiteley P (2012) Political participation in Britain – the decline and revival of civic culture. Palgrave MacMillan, Basingstoke

Zeier K, Grün G (2025) German election results explained in graphics. Deutsche Welle. Accessed 27 Feb 2025

Chapter 5
Executive Accountability

Abstract The ability of people to fulfil their role as citizens depends on their being able to obtain information relating to the government's performance so as to hold it to account. One way in which these objectives are served is by parliament acting on behalf of voters and using the powers it has under the doctrine of responsible government to inquire into the conduct of the executive and to express lack of confidence in ministers. However these powers are less effective in practice than they are in theory. One reason for this is that the doctrine of parliamentary privilege, specifically Article 9 of the Bill of Rights Act of 1689, which has widely been adopted throughout the Commonwealth and which denies the courts jurisdiction to inquire into parliamentary proceedings. This means that no recourse is available in instances where members of the executive either refuse to attend parliamentary committees that are seeking to question them or, even if they do attend, refuse to answer questions. In addition, the ability of parliamentary committees to initiate contempt proceedings in such circumstances is circumscribed by the fact that such proceedings must be initiated by parliament as a whole where, by definition, the government has a majority. This also makes it virtually impossible for an adverse finding relating to a minister's performance to lead to a vote of no confidence. This chapter argues that the law should be reformed in such a way as to make it an offence to refuse to attend a parliamentary committee or to give evidence to it, giving the courts the jurisdiction to hear such cases and conferring standing on individual committee members to initiate proceedings. This would overcome the problem of governmental control over contempt process and would ensure that citizens have access to the information they need to make informed decisions.

5.1 Executive Accountability

The capacity of citizens to make decisions pertaining to public affairs, depends in large part on their ability to obtain information about the government's performance and to hold it to account. In parliamentary systems, one of the ways in which this is achieved is by parliamentary committees using their inquiry power. Yet a constant

B. Harris, *Cultivating Good Citizenship*,
SpringerBriefs in Law, https://doi.org/10.1007/978-981-92-2740-2_5

source of peoples' dissatisfaction with the political system is lack of accountability on the part of the executive, which indicates that the system of legislative scrutiny of the executive is failing and in need of reform. The reason for this lies in the way in which the law of parliamentary privilege has developed, and the paradox that a legal rule that sought to preserve the rights of parliament in the face of abuse of power by the executive now impedes the ability of parliament to hold the executive accountable.

5.2 Parliamentary Privilege

The law of parliamentary privilege consists of common law principles, statutes and parliament's own internal rules which, in the case of the United Kingdom, accumulated over many centuries. The key development arose out of the conflict between crown and parliament in the seventeenth century. The conflict between the two branches of government became increasingly acrimonious and during the reign of Charles I, who ordered that members of parliament who had expressed opposition to his policies be arrested and tried for sedition.[1] The conflict ended with the Glorious Revolution of 1688, when parliament expelled James II and invited William of Orange and Mary Stuart to rule as joint monarchs, on condition that they consent to terms regulating the relationship between crown and parliament contained in the Bill of Rights 1689. Article 9 of the Bill of Rights provided that

> The Freedom of Speech and Debates or Proceedings in Parliament ought not to be impeached or questioned in any Court or Place out of Parliament.

The effect of this provision was to protect freedom of speech, as well as the conduct of parliamentary business more generally, from outside interference, in an obvious reaction to monarchical practices earlier in the century. Importantly, although the purpose of Article 9 was to curb the power of the executive in the person of the monarch, it did that by denying the courts jurisdiction to hear cases involving anything occurring during the course of parliamentary proceedings, because it was through the avenue of prosecutions before the courts that the monarchy had intimidated its political opponents. The most well-known example of the operation of Article 9 is that a plaintiff who alleges that they have been defamed by an MP (or indeed anyone else) during the course of parliamentary proceedings is barred from bringing an action, because doing so would require the courts to hear evidence of, and thus inquire into, what was said during parliamentary proceedings.

The immunity contained in Article 9 is just one of the many rules of parliamentary privilege in accordance with which parliament regulates how it operates. The key point is that that regulation occurs free from oversight by any external authority. This body of law, including Article 9 or re-enactments of it, applies not only in the United

---

[1] *R v Eliot, Hollis and Valentine* (1629) 3 St Tr 294.

Kingdom but also in many other countries that inherited the parliamentary model of government.

While there are differences between jurisdictions, it is generally true that parliamentary privilege includes the power of parliament and its committees to conduct inquiries and to summons people to give evidence and produce documents, as well as the power to punish people for contempt, broadly defined as any conduct that interferes with the workings of parliament—which includes failure to appear before committees and answer questions. Depending on the particular jurisdiction, a parliament may have the power to arrest, fine or even imprison those who defy its will. On the face of it, these powers seem to put parliament in a powerful position. However, several factors have led to these powers becoming more apparent than real.

5.3 Factors Undermining Executive Accountability

Parliament's seventeenth century assertion of its privileges was directed towards the commendable objective of ensuring that it was protected against interference by the executive. However, three factors combined to lead to a quite different and unpredicted outcome, one which has led to parliament becoming subordinate to the executive, and the executive escaping effective scrutiny by parliament.

5.3.1 The Transfer of Control Over Executive Power from Monarch to Parliament

The first development was a shift in executive power from the monarch to parliament itself. In the decades following the Glorious Revolution, a convention developed that, instead of exercising day to day executive power him or herself, the monarch left control of government to ministers that had the support of, and were responsible to, parliament. What the development of 'parliamentary' or 'responsible' government meant in practice was that the monarch would choose as prime minister the person who was able to command a majority in the House of Commons and that person would advise the monarch who to appoint to other cabinet positions. Tying the monarch's choice to whoever had a majority in the House was a practical necessity, because only a government that could secure passage of its legislation, in particular legislation authorising taxation and expenditure, would be able to function. The government was 'responsible' to parliament in the sense that it held power only so long as it was able to retain majority support, and if parliament expressed dissatisfaction in a minister, that person would, by convention, have to resign. The importance of the change in locus of executive power cannot be overstated, because it meant that executive and legislative power were now fused. Instead of being a source of power lying outside parliament, the executive, in the person of the prime minister and other ministers, was now located within parliament and, at least initially, was controlled by it.

5.3.2 The Growth of the Party System

The second factor was the reversal of the balance of power between parliament and the executive. At first blush the system that emerged in the wake of the Glorious Revolution appeared to place parliament firmly in control of the executive headed by ministers drawn from its own membership (albeit with the monarch remaining as a purely formal source of executive authority). However, the relationship between MPs and those of their number who were members of the cabinet underwent a radical change from the late nineteenth century. Whereas in the seventeenth and eighteenth centuries party formations were loose and many MPs had no party affiliation, from the late nineteenth century mass democratisation and the increasing expense of elections meant candidates hoping to win election needed the support of a party machine which expected their loyalty in return. This led to an increasingly rigid party system in which the leadership of the governing party—in other words the cabinet—used the threat of disendorsement as a means of exerting control over their own MPs. The consequence of this was that whereas in the seventeenth and eighteenth centuries the cabinet (both collectively and individually) lived in apprehension of losing the support of parliament, by the twentieth century MPs lived in apprehension of what would happen if they disobeyed their party leadership—a sure way of which would be to express lack of confidence in the government of their own party or one of its ministers. This means that parliament—where the government by definition has a majority which it controls through party discipline—is highly unlikely to force a minister to resign for misconduct.

5.3.3 Majority Party Control Over the Exercise of Contempt Powers

This brings one to the third factor that undermined parliamentary scrutiny of the executive, which is that the rules of parliamentary privilege do not permit committees acting on their own to use parliament's coercive powers against those who refuse to co-operate with its investigations. The previous paragraph discussed the unlikelihood of a minister facing a vote of no confidence. In reality, matters rarely progress to that point. The weakness of parliament in the face of the executive usually manifests itself before that, at the stage when a parliamentary committee attempts to obtain information from the executive.

As already noted, the law of parliamentary privilege confers investigative powers on committees, including those of requesting witnesses to appear, answer questions and produce documents. The scope of these powers varies widely between jurisdictions.[2] In the case of the United Kingdom, committees do not have the power to summons MPs or government ministers, but can request their attendance.[3] The same is true in Australia.[4] By contrast, the Scottish Parliament, the Northern Ireland Assembly and the Welsh Senedd may require any person, including ministers, to appear before committees, failure to do so being an offence.[5] However, as is discussed below, even if a person can be compelled to appear, whether accountability is achieved depends on who has the power to determine whether those who refuse to appear will be proceeded against for contempt.

Even if the law does require cabinet ministers and public servants to attend committees, the committee may find itself facing different problem of a witness refusing to answer questions. Failure to attend a committee when summonsed or to comply with requests for information *prima facie* amount to contempt of parliament. However, in parliamentary systems, the power to punish for contempt vests in the legislative chamber as a whole—not in individual committees. Therefore, a committee which alleges that a minister has refused to attend or give evidence must refer the matter to the house to decide whether to impose a sanction for contempt. But since the government has a majority in the legislature, it is a foregone conclusion that no action will be taken. The same occurs even in circumstances where a committee has succeeded in discovering ministerial maladministration, corruption or illegality and submits a report to that effect to parliament—the government will use its majority to prevent action being taken against one of its own.

Compliance with rules of behaviour is ultimately determined by political culture. This is particularly so in parliamentary systems, where important rules governing the relationship between the legislature and the executive, as well as behavioural norms—such as those contained in the Cabinet Manual and the Ministerial Code in the case of the United Kingdom—take the form of legally unenforceable conventions rather than rules of law, compliance with which is reliant on political operators 'doing the right thing' and having sufficient conscience to resign if they have breached rules of conduct.[6] In countries where there is a social expectation that the rules will be complied with, they generally are. By contrast, in countries where the public has become inured to departures from rules, they gradually lose their force until they become empty, and the vulnerability of the system becomes evident. Convention-based systems worked when politicians, particularly those from the party in power, are prepared to enforce standards, but the reality is that in many countries there is no standard other than what serves the objective of retaining power. Whether a minister resigns or not now depends entirely on whether the degree of public embarrassment

---

[2] For a survey of the position in select jurisdictions see House of Commons Committee of Privileges (2021, pp. 59–64).

[3] Hutton et al. (2019, ¶ 38.34).

[4] Elder and Fowler (2018, pp. 702–3).

[5] See ss 23 and 25 of the *Scotland Act 1998*, ss 44 and 45 of the *Northern Ireland Act 1998* and ss 37 and 39 of the *Government of Wales Act* 2006.

[6] Sargeant et al. (2023, pp. 16, 19–22, 73–5).

they have caused the government is such as to make it politically expedient for the Prime Minister to ask for their resignation.

The current state of the doctrine of responsible government was succinctly summarised by the late Harry Evans, Clerk of the Senate in Australia who said[7]:

> Responsible government was a system which existed from the mid-19th century to the early 20th century, after which it disappeared. It involved a lower house of parliament with the ability to dismiss a government and appoint another between elections. This system has been replaced by one whereby the government of the day controls the lower house by a built-in, totally reliable and "rusted on" majority. Not only is the government not responsible to, that is, removable by, the lower house, but it is also not accountable to it. The government's control of the parliamentary processes means that it is never effectively called to account...

The conclusion one reaches is that because of the combined effect of the emergence of responsible government, the development of a rigid party system and the rule that only parliament, and not its committees, can initiate contempt proceedings, the coercive power of parliament—and thus its capacity to hold the executive accountable—is now theoretical rather than real. Whereas on the one hand the rules of parliamentary privilege grant parliament the power to scrutinise their executive, on the other they make the government of the day gatekeeper over whether that scrutiny is in fact possible.

Since Article 9 of the Bill of Rights 1689 prohibits the courts from inquiring into parliamentary proceedings, there is no other avenue available to a parliamentary committee seeking to enforce executive accountability. The result is that despite its origins as a defence of parliament from executive tyranny, Article 9 now provides a shield the executive can use to prevent scrutiny of its actions by parliament. The transfer of real executive power from the person of the monarch to the cabinet meant that far from heralding the liberation of parliament, the 1689 constitutional settlement would ultimately lead to is subjugation. The question that must be addressed is what institutional reform would re-establish parliamentary control over the executive as the system of responsible government originally promised.

5.4 Creating an Effective System of Government Accountability

No-one should be their own regulator. This principle applies with particular force to governments, yet the way the parliamentary system has evolved, which enables governing parties to use their parliamentary majority to avoid scrutiny, has the result of making governments the arbitrators of whether and how much information they will disclose to parliament. It also and means that a legal question—whether a contempt in the form of refusing to make such disclosure has occurred—is decided by a political rather than by a legal body and, moreover, is almost always decided along political lines.

[7] Evans (2002).

The solution to the problem is obvious—conferral on the courts of the jurisdiction to compel executive compliance with requests by parliamentary committees to attend and to give evidence. This would obviously necessitate legislation creating an exception to Article 9. Article 9 has never amounted to a complete prohibition on the courts inquiring into what occurs in parliament. A well-established exception is the need of the courts to refer to parliamentary speeches when interpreting legislation.[8] Another is where the question arises as to whether parliament has complied with constitutionally-mandated procedural requirements for the enactment of legislation.[9] It would seem to be equally justifiable to create an exception directed towards re-establishing executive accountability to parliament, which is what the system of parliamentary government is supposedly founded upon.

A change to committee powers was mooted in the United Kingdom in 2021, when the House of Commons Committee of Privileges published a report that recommended that legislation be introduced to create a criminal offence of failure to attend a committee to answer questions, with prosecution being initiated by referral to the courts by the Speaker of the House of Commons, acting in accordance with a resolution by the house.[10] Unfortunately, the report attracted significant opposition, and in its next report the Committee revised its recommendations and the draft bill so as to provide that the offence it created would relate only to failure to attend a committee or to provide documents and would not make it an offence to refuse to answer questions—an amendment which denied the proposal much of its force.[11] The Committee also revised the bill so as to state that it would not apply to members of either house of parliament, arguing that MPs who refused to attend committees were already subject to the jurisdiction of the house[12]—an argument which ignores the fact that government control over the house is the key impediment to ministerial accountability. In the event, the draft bill was not introduced and the powers of committees were left as they had been. A similar proposal introduced into parliament in Australia by a minor party senator in 1994 would have made it a criminal offence to fail to comply with an order of a house or a committee. However the bill was not proceeded with due to opposition by the major parties.[13]

Assuming that the law was changed to create an offence of non-attendance at or non-cooperation with a parliamentary committee, a key factor which would determine the efficacy of the law would be who had standing to report a breach of privilege and thus initiate criminal proceedings. Leaving that to parliament as a whole would simply replicate the problem of government control over when remedies can be

[8] In Australia this exception to the statutory version of Article 9 is contained in s 16(5)(b) of the *Parliamentary Privileges Act 1989* (Cth). Authority for the exception in the United Kingdom is found in *Pepper v Hart* [1993] AC 593.

[9] In Australia see s 16(5)(b) of the *Parliamentary Privileges Act 1989* (Cth). In the United Kingdom see *Jackson v Attorney-General* [2006] 1 AC 262.

[10] House of Commons Committee of Privileges (2021, pp. 46–9, 65–6).

[11] House of Commons Committee of Privileges (2022, pp. 20, 37–8).

[12] House of Commons Committee of Privileges (2022, pp. 29–30, 37–8).

[13] Parliament of Australia (1994).

brought against it. Even leaving it to a committee as a whole would not work in circumstances where, as is common in many parliamentary systems, the composition of committees mirrors party standing in the house from which the committee is drawn, thus giving governing parties a majority on committees.[14] For these reasons, the law should state that any individual member of a committee should have the powers to summons witnesses and require them to answer questions and, in the event of non-compliance, be able to initiate a criminal complaint for contempt.

A defence of noncompliance due to reasonable excuse should be available. An obvious circumstance would be where public interest immunity applied—for example, where a parliamentary committee sought information that could not be disclosed on national security grounds or where cabinet confidentiality and the freedom it gives the government to debate policy in private militates against public disclosure. This does not mean that a mere assertion of public interest immunity should suffice, as indeed is the current position where governments routinely cite this as a reason for refusing to share information with committees but without adducing reasons as to *why* immunity should apply. This is yet another example of a legal question being decided by a political body. A reformed law of parliamentary privilege should therefore provide that it is up to the courts to determine whether public interest immunity justifies the withholding of information from a committee.

An example of how such cases are decided is provided by the United States where, paradoxically, despite the doctrine of separation of powers, the executive is subject to far greater oversight by the legislature than in countries with parliamentary systems of government where the executive is fused (at cabinet level) with the legislature and, in theory, is answerable to it. In *United States v Nixon*,[15] the Supreme Court balanced the right of congressional committees to obtain information from the executive against the doctrine of separation of powers, which limits the extent to which each branch of government can involve itself in the workings of the others. In accordance with longstanding precedent that Congress has a right to investigate the conduct of the executive—including cabinet members[16]—the court held that the executive cannot be compelled to give information if the possibility that communications would be subject to disclosure would impair the confidentiality and candour of policy deliberations.[17] However, the court explicitly stated that a mere claim of privilege is not determinative—it will be up to the courts to determine whether the claim is justified.[18] In doing so, the courts would balance the interest to be served by disclosing the information against the reasons for the executive's claim to confidentiality.[19] The

[14] In the case of the UK see Hutton et al. (2019, ¶ 39.3), for Australia see Elder and Fowler (2018, p. 659).

[15] 418 US 683 (1974) 705.

[16] *Anderson v Dunn* 19 TS (6 Wheat.) 204 (1821); *McGrain v Daugherty* 273 US 135 (1927).

[17] 418 US 683 (1974) 705, 708.

[18] 418 US 683 (1974), 703.

[19] 418 US 683 (1974), 711–12. See also *Senate Select Committee on Presidential Campaign Activities v Nixon* 498 F.2d 725 (D.C. Cir 1974) and *United States v A T & T* 521 F.2d 384 (D.C. Cir 1976) and 567 F. 2d 121 (D.C. Cir 1977).

court held that even in a case where a claim of privilege is based on national security, the executive must satisfy the court that that issue is involved, if necessary by providing evidence to the court *in camera*.[20] The Supreme Court reaffirmed these rules in *Nixon v Administrator of General Services*,[21] in which it held that there was no blanket right to executive privilege,[22] and that claim of privilege would succeed only where the executive could show that disclosure would significantly impair its ability to achieve its constitutional function.[23]

The fact that referral to the courts is possible means that the executive defers to Congress and that the powers of the executive and legislative branches are balanced in a way that under parliamentary systems they are not. As a consequence, it is usual for cabinet members to appear before congressional committees and for disagreements over what should be disclosed to them to settled by negotiation between the two branches,[24] often involving an agreement that the executive will provide evidence in a closed session of a committee.[25]

The example of the United States demonstrates that it is possible to balance the powers of the legislature, executive and judiciary in such a way as to ensure effective legislative oversight of the executive, thereby enabling citizens to evaluate the actions of the government.

5.5 Executive Accountability and Citizen Engagement

Access to information is a prerequisite for citizens' ability to make informed decisions. While there may be other mechanisms, such as freedom of information processes, that may enable this, these are usually subject to exclusions and restrictions and, in any event, put on the citizen the burden of going through what might be a prolonged administrative process. The ability of parliament to discover information on behalf of the public provides a more direct avenue of ensuring transparency on the part of the government.

The extent to which a parliament has the power to extract information also determines the degree of accountability that can be imposed on the executive. This also

---

20 418 US 683 (1974), 713–14.

21 433 US 425 (1977).

22 433 US 425 (1977), 446–7.

23 433 US 425 (1977), 443.

24 Marshall (2004, pp. 806–8), Fisher (2002, p. 325).

25 Rozell (1994, p. 150).

has a direct impact on levels of citizen engagement in public affairs as lack of executive accountability has a corrosive effect on the conduct of government and therefore on public confidence in the political system,[26] which in turn reduces political participation.[27] As Whiteley states[28]

> If most citizens think that politicians are corrupt or in it for what they can get, and the institutions they serve weak or venal, then they are likely to ignore politics altogether or try to undermine government processes. If these views are widespread in society then democracy will not function effectively. Thus the values and beliefs that citizens have about their own political system and their role in it are crucial to the effectiveness of democratic politics.

In instances where citizens do remain politically engaged, unaddressed corruption makes voters ripe for exploitation by populists.[29]

By contrast, effective scrutiny of government increases trust in public institutions[30] and fosters willingness to participate in political processes,[31] thereby enhancing the opportunity for, and quality of, citizen engagement. The mechanics of the internal workings of parliament may seem arcane, but they are critical to the ability of the legislature to hold the executive accountable for its actions and thereby to maintain citizen confidence in the system of government.

References

Diamond (2025) The political drivers of low trust. Open Government Partnership, Washington DC

Elder D, Fowler P (eds) (2018) House of representatives practice, 7th edn. Department of the House of Representatives, Canberra

Evans H (2002) The Australian parliament: time for reformation. Address to the National Press Club, 24 April 2002 https://australianpolitics.com/2002/04/24/harry-evans-parliamentary-reform-speech.html. Accessed 4 July 2025

Fisher L (2002) Congressional access to information: using legislative will and leverage. Duke Law J 52(2002):323–402

House of Commons Committee of Privileges (2021) Select committees and contempts: clarifying and strengthening powers to call for persons, papers and records – First Report of Session 2019–21. House of Commons, London

House of Commons Committee of Privileges (2022) Select committees and contempts: review of consultation on Committee proposals – First Report of Session 2022–23. House of Commons, London

Hutton J, Natzler D, Hamlyn M, Lee C, Mawson C, Poyser C, Samson E, Lawrence K (2019) Erskine may: parliamentary practice, 25th edn. Lexis-Nexis, London

Kartal M (2025) The (unintended) consequences of ineffective corruption control on populism in Europe. West Eur Politics 48:1428–55

[26] Diamond (2025).

[27] Olsson (2014, pp. 8–9).

[28] Whiteley (2012, p. 15).

[29] Kartal (2025, pp. 1436–9).

[30] OECD (2025, pp. 16, 27).

[31] White (2015, p. 11).

Marshall W (2004) The limits on congress's authority to investigate the President. Univ Illinois Law Rev 781–825
Olsson S (2014) Corruption and political participation: a multilevel analysis. University of Gothenburg, Gothenburg
Organisation for Economic Co-operation and Development (2025) Recommendation of the council on open government. OECD, Paris
Parliament of Australia (1994) Report – Senate standing committee on privileges. Parliament of the Commonwealth of Australia, Canberra
Rozell M (1994) Executive privilege: the dilemma of secrecy and democratic accountability. Johns Hopkins Press, Baltimore
Sargeant A, Coulter S, Pannell J, McKee R, Hynes M (2023) Review of the UK constitution - final report. Institute for Government, London
White H (2015) Parliamentary scrutiny of government. Institute for Government, London
Whiteley P (2012) Political participation in Britain – the decline and revival of civic culture. Palgrave MacMillan, Basingstoke

Chapter 6
Political Leaders and Good Citizenship

Abstract Surveys in many countries indicate a significant loss of public confidence in politicians, which is unsurprising given several recent scandals involving abuse of power. This has led to widespread public disillusionment with, and disconnection from, political processes. However, in democracies at least, the fact that citizens elect politicians whose ethical shortcomings are notorious makes them partly responsible for this state of affairs. While it is true that citizens are entitled to vote in accordance with their personal interests, good citizenship requires that citizens take the public interest into account when exercising their vote. This may mean voting for a candidate they prefer less but whose values and behaviour make them more worthy of office. Good citizenship also requires that, politicians should balance their own sectional political interests with those of society as a whole when exercising power, which may require adopting a course of action that is politically disadvantageous. Given their position of power and advantage, politicians are under a particular obligation to foster knowledge of civics. Unfortunately, some politicians find it politically advantageous to discourage citizens from becoming informed and instead propagate misinformation and disinformation. This was particularly evident in Australia during constitutional referenda in 1999 and 2023, leading some commentators to advocate truth in political advertising legislation which would criminalise false or misleading statements made during election or referendum campaigns. However, the creation of an official political 'truth' is incompatible with freedom of expression and, more fundamentally, with Mill's sceptical epistemology discussed in Chap. 1, which recognises that since it is not possible conclusively to state that something is true, suppressing a statement because it is considered untrue is to claim infallibility, and that the search for truth is enhanced by an encountering error. Political decision-making is an inescapable burden of citizenship and cannot be avoided by vesting in the state the power to determine what is true and untrue. The chapter concludes by arguing that the discussion of good citizenship reveals the limits of law: Law is a coercive system. It is also reactive—its power is felt after it has been breached when a sanction is imposed. By contrast, the values and practices of good citizenship are founded on a voluntary internal commitment resulting in proactive behaviours benefitting society.

B. Harris, *Cultivating Good Citizenship*,
SpringerBriefs in Law, https://doi.org/10.1007/978-981-92-2740-2_6

6.1 Disillusionment with Political Leaders

Negative public perception of the conduct of politicians is notorious. In the United Kingdom a 2024 survey by the National Centre for Social Research found that 45% of respondents would 'almost never' trust British governments to place the needs of the nation above the interests of their own party, and that 58% would 'almost never' trust politicians of any party in Britain to tell the truth when they are in a tight corner.[1] In the United States a poll published in 2025 by the National Opinion Research Centre found that only two in 10 respondents trust government officials to do the right thing, while seven in 10 believed that corporations and the wealthy control the government.[2]

In Australia a 2022 survey found that only 30% of respondents considered that politicians could be trusted, 70% believed that politicians were in politics to look after themselves, 54% believed that politicians served big interests and only 12% that politicians served the interests of ordinary people.[3] Similarly, a 2023 survey found that 49% of respondents agreed with the statement that 'corruption is widespread in Australia's institutions and processes.'[4] These sentiments have led to voters feeling that they are powerless—and, more concerningly, according to the results of a 2024 survey on populism, have led 52% of Australian respondents to believe that the country needs a 'strong leader willing to break the rules.'[5]

There is ample reason for voters to feel resentment towards political actors. Among some of the most recent in the UK was the reappointment of Suella Braverman as Home Secretary just six days after she had been forced to resign because of her breach of the ministerial code of conduct by using a personal email account to send official documents.[6] Public confidence in politicians was also undermined by revelations of a culture of bullying and harassment in parliament contained in a report published in 2018,[7] and remains a serious problem as evidenced by the fact that complaints increased by 40% in the year to April 2025.[8]

Recent scandals in Australia include a blatant campaign of pork-barrelling when the government distributed $ 100 million in funds allocated for sports facilities to projects situated in electorates it held, or marginal electorates that it hoped to win at the upcoming general election, rather than in accordance with the merit-based ranking that had been provided by an independent commission.[9] Even more serious in its consequences was what became known as the 'robodebt' scandal where the same government was found to have devised and implemented an illegal policy under

---

[1] Curtice, Montagu and Sivathasan (2024, p. 4).

[2] Rosentiel (2025).

[3] Cameron and McAllister (2022, pp. 101–2).

[4] Australian Public Service Commission (2023, p. 13).

[5] Ipsos (2024).

[6] Francis (2022).

[7] Cox (2018).

[8] Mitchell (2025).

[9] Harris (2023a, pp. 45–9).

which welfare entitlements were calculated by a software programme rather than by human assessment. The programme automatically issued letters which incorrectly stated that recipients had claimed payments they were not entitled to—sometimes in amounts of tens of thousands of dollars—for which they were then sued. The government persisted in using the scheme even after ministers had been advised that the policy was unlawful[10] and that the IT programme was flawed.[11] The most terrible consequence of the scheme was the fact that a number of welfare recipients pursued for debt took their own lives.[12] In Australia too a culture of bullying in parliament became starkly evident in 2018 when supporters of one of the candidates for the Liberal party leadership bullied MPs into voting for him.[13]

Resentment of leaders' conduct is particularly deep in cases which disclose an attitude by politicians that they are exempt from complying with the law. A striking example of this is provided by former UK Prime Minister Boris Johnson's claim that he was unaware that it was illegal under the COVID regulations—promulgated by his own government—to hold social events at his residence in Downing Street, which led to his being found to have deliberately misled parliament.[14] Defiance of the law was also evident in Donald Trump's alleged pressuring of the Georgia Secretary of State to find him 11 000 additional votes during counting after the 2020 presidential election,[15] and his alleged incitement of the insurrection of 6 January 2021.[16] Misconduct by leaders has consequences beyond those of the unlawful acts themselves: It leads to a progressive erosion of standards to the point where voters suffer from scandal fatigue, their sensibilities become blunted and misbehaviour and corruption are seen as a normal part of politics.[17] People follow the example set by their leaders, so misbehaviour by the latter, particularly when engaged in with impunity, undermines the ethics of society as a whole, making citizens themselves more likely to engage in unlawful conduct.[18]

Accepting that bad behaviour by politicians is inconsistent with good citizenship and diminishes public confidence in government, what is the remedy? Voter resentment of politicians has an element of hypocrisy unless voters acknowledge their own responsibility for those politicians' ascent to power. So, in order to determine what can be done to improve political standards, it is necessary to consider the relative responsibility for poor political culture of politicians and of the voters who elect them.

---

[10] Royal Commission into the Robodebt Scheme (2023, pp. 26–7, 42, 271–9).

[11] Royal Commission into the Robodebt Scheme (2023, pp. 170, 176).

[12] Royal Commission into the Robodebt Scheme (2023, pp. 337–40).

[13] Murphy (2018).

[14] House of Commons Committee of Privileges (2023).

[15] Sullivan (2021).

[16] Cabral (2021).

[17] Luce (2024).

[18] Marien and Hooge (2011, pp. 271–3, 281–3).

6.2 Voters' Responsibility for Bad Leadership

Like all truisms, the statement that in a democracy people get the political leaders they deserve is an over-simplification containing an element of truth. The question of who bears responsibility for political leaders' behaviour needs to be broken down into two components: how voters decide who to vote for, and the way in which elected leaders exercise power.

Data on what motivates voter decision-making is voluminous. Predictably it reveals that the attention of voters is self-interested, primarily focussing on issues they consider most important. In the 2024 presidential election in the United States, 21% of respondents to a survey ranked performance of the economy was of greatest concern to them, followed by 13% who cited immigration and 9% who cited abortion and reproductive rights.[19] During the 2024 United Kingdom general election, 45% of respondents prioritised the cost of living, 34% health care and 32% the economy on general.[20] Similarly, prior to the 2025 federal election in Australia, 57% of respondents gave greatest weight to the cost of living, 31% to health and 23% to crime.[21] None of this data is surprising. Nor is there anything wrong with voters voting in accordance with self-interest—that is what democracy empowers them to do.

However what is significant about these priorities is the absence of concern about the character of politicians. Even if one looks further down the list of issues in the surveys cited above, matters connected—even indirectly—to character attract a low level of concern. In the USA ethics, morals, decency and honesty were prioritised by 5% of voters as was the character of candidates. In Australia, open and honest government was of concern to 19% of voters, while in the UK integrity of politicians was not mentioned. It was usually only when respondents were specifically asked to rank the relative trustworthiness of specific politicians that their focus was directed towards issues of character.

How does one reconcile voter disdain for the behaviour of politicians discussed in Part 1 of this chapter with their evident disinterest in character issues when they go to the polls, made obvious by the fact that even in instances where candidates are of notoriously bad character, they nevertheless succeed in being elected? Boris Johnson became prime minister notwithstanding a long history of lying, starting when he was dismissed from his position at the *London Times* for fabricated journalism.[22] Donald Trump won the 2016 presidential election despite the release of an audio tape in which he boasted of random sexual assaults of women[23] and despite numerous women coming forward to complain of such behaviour.[24] He won the 2024 election despite having been found civilly liable for sexual assault[25] and being convicted of

[19] Brennan (2024).

[20] Smith (2024).

[21] Roy Morgan (2025).

[22] Grierson (2021).

[23] Timm (2016).

[24] Cleal (2024).

[25] McGreal and Pengelly (2023).

breaching electoral law.[26] Peter Dutton became prime minister of Australia despite making racist comments about migrants of African[27] and Lebanese descent[28] and stating that it was 'un-Australian' for lawyers to represent refugees.[29] These examples could be multiplied many times over and from many countries, but they illustrate the same point, which is that voters subordinate considerations of worthiness for office to voting for whoever they believe will best serve their personal interests, and must therefore accept ultimate responsibility for the fact that they find politicians to be untrustworthy. This is a hard truth, but it contains the important lesson that voter complaints about the standard of political leadership to some extent rings hollow because improvement in the standard of politics lies in the hands of voters themselves.

How then should a voter balance a candidate's ability—or rather promise—to implement policies serving the voter's interests against the candidate's suitability for office as revealed by their character? Here it is instructive to refer back to the discussion of civic republicanism discussed in Chap. 1, in which it was noted that according to Cicero, good citizenship required that a citizen act not solely in accordance with self-interest but also in accordance with the common good, and to prioritise the common good over personal interests when the two were in conflict.[30] When applied to voting, the equal importance that civic republicanism places on individualism and communitarianism means that whereas a voter undoubtedly has the right to vote selfishly—to use a harsh term—good citizenship may, depending on the circumstances, require them to vote against their own interests if the candidate they prefer has character flaws that make them unfit for office. Of course, whether a candidate's character meets that threshold will be a matter of degree. It is unusual for a candidate to have no personal shortcomings, but the recent examples given above of political leaders in the USA, the UK are ones where character defects were both obvious and severe, and the success of these leaders indicates a failure on the part of voters to temper their choices by reference to the common good.

However the problem is that whereas determining where one's self interest lies is relatively easy, determining what serves the common good requires a level of analysis many voters are not capable of. Apart from that, societies face the paradox that in an age of almost limitless information and multiple platforms on which that information can be communicated, it has become more difficult and time-consuming to determine the reliability of sources and thereby to engage in such analysis. The result, as noted in Chap. 3, is that many voters rely on sources that are not subject to journalistic rigour and which present material in simplistic or emotional terms. This means that even people who are willing to make an effort to discovering what lies in the public interest fall victim to misinformation and disinformation. One should in passing mention that the dichotomy between what is in the interest of the individual

[26] Bustillo and Bernstein (2024).

[27] Karp (2018).

[28] Anderson (2016).

[29] Hall (2017).

[30] Bufacchi (2023, p. 41).

and what is in the interest of society as a whole is ultimately false, because a society in which the public interest is consistently ignored will eventually fail, harming the personal interests of the individuals who comprise it, but unfortunately many voters do not take a sufficiently long term view to realise this.

All this highlights the importance of a system of civics education which instils in future voters the values of civic republicanism as well as the intellectual capacity to engage in analysis of public affairs. So, while it is correct to say that, in a democracy, voters bear ultimate responsibility for the shortcomings of their leaders, that responsibility is mitigated where they have not received an adequate education in citizenship and civics.

6.3 Political Leadership and the Demands of Civic Republicanism

To appreciate the requirements that good citizenship imposes on leaders, it is first necessary to understand the basis of the relationship between leaders and those who elect them. This is not one of agency with the leader's exercise of power confined to an obligation to implement the wishes of the specific segment of the electorate who elected him or her, but is rather based on the idea that a leader is elected for their capacity to exercise discretion. The most frequently cited expression of this principle was that by Edmund Burke in his *Speech to the Electors of Bristol* in 1774[31]:

> Your representative owes you, not his industry only, but his judgment; and he betrays, instead of serving you, if he sacrifices it to your opinion...
>
> To deliver an opinion, is the right of all men; that of constituents is a weighty and respectable opinion, which a representative ought always to rejoice to hear; and which he ought always most seriously to consider. But authoritative *instructions*; *mandates* issued, which the member is bound blindly and implicitly to obey, to vote, and to argue for, though contrary to the clearest conviction of his judgment and conscience; these are things utterly unknown to the laws of this land, and which arise from a fundamental mistake of the whole order and tenour of our constitution.
>
> Parliament is not a *congress* of ambassadors from different and hostile interests; which interests each must maintain, as an agent and advocate, against other agents and advocates; but parliament is a *deliberative* assembly of *one* nation, with *one* interest, that of the whole; where, not local purposes, not local prejudices, ought to guide, but the general good, resulting from the general reason of the whole. You choose a member indeed; but when you have chosen him, he is not member of Bristol, but he is a member of *parliament*. If the local constituent should have an interest, or should form an hasty opinion, evidently opposite to the real good of the rest of the community, the member for that place ought to be as far, as any other, from any endeavour to give it effect. (Emphasis in the original).

This speech is notable not only for its articulation of the role of the leader in a democracy but also for its clarity in rejecting the view, still expressed nowadays, that a government is, or ought to be, circumscribed in its action by the policies on which

---

[31] Burke (1777, pp. 353–4).

it was elected—commonly referred to as its 'election mandate.' While breach of election promises might be thought of as a prime example of conduct that contributes to public disillusionment with politicians, practical considerations indicate why the mandate model is flawed: The exigencies that a government must respond to make it unrealistic for it either blindly to pursue policies that are no longer in the public interest or to call an election every time it needs to depart from the platform on which it was elected. Indeed, contrary to the view that departing from election promises breaches the public trust, not to do so where a government determines that it is necessary would breach the trust reposed in government as custodian of the national interest, would prioritise retaining popularity over the public interest and would prioritise the interests of the particular segment of the voting population who voted the government into power over the interests of the citizen body as a whole. The Burkean concept of the politician as repository of discretion to be exercised in the interests of the nation as a whole accords with the ideas underlying civic republicanism—even if he would most likely have rejected his ideas being characterised in that way.

When applied to individual politicians, the fact that the civic republican concept of leadership requires subordination of personal advantage to the common good means that the circumstances may be such as to require a leader to act to their own political *disadvantage*. Unfortunately, this idea is alien to most political leaders and would most likely be thought of as naïve. Yet it marks the difference between a statesman or woman and a mere politician. Two examples are provided by Winston Churchill, who was a rising figure in the Conservative party early in his career but crossed the floor to the Liberals because of his belief that the policy of protectionism which had been adopted by the Conservatives, was harmful to the poor.[32] Churchill later re-joined the Conservatives, but again acted to his political detriment by condemning appeasement of Nazi Germany, which led him to being excluded from public office by the party hierarchy during most of the 1930s.[33]

More recently, Mikhail Gorbachev reversed decades of policy by surrendering the monopoly of political power held by the of communist party in the USSR, dismantling an oppressive system that had existed for 70 years.[34] South African president F W De Klerk acted contrary to his party's own sectional and ideological interests by unbanning the African National Congress, freeing political prisoners, dismantling the legislative edifice of apartheid and beginning a process of negotiations that led to the holding of the first election in which all South Africans were entitled to vote.[35] What is significant about both Gorbachev and De Klerk is that they led rather than followed: Having entered political life as firm adherents of their oppressive ideologies, they took enormous personal political risks by adopting policies that were adverse to their own parties' interests and used their persuasive powers to convince their supporters of the need to accept radical change.

---

[32] Gilbert (1981, pp. 27–33).

[33] Addison (2006, p. 131).

[34] Galeotti (1997, pp. 87, 110–12, 122–3).

[35] Gilomee (2013, pp. 328–52).

However, these examples are exceptional. Politics more usually reflects one or other of two negative trends: Politicians either follow voters rather than leading them, campaigning on election platforms designed to attract support while avoiding policies which voters will find difficult to accept, even if they are necessary. The other trend is one in which politicians neither lead voters nor follow them but rather manipulate voters into wanting what is in politicians' interests for them to want. Under this model, politics degenerates into marketing, a fundamental principle of which is that it is more advantageous for a seller to create a new demand rather than to satisfy an existing one. Neither of these models is consistent with civic republicanism, which acknowledges the tension that exists between the duty of the leader to be responsive to the will of the voters and their duty to act in the interests of society as a whole. This tension is resolved by the recognition that good leadership involves more than giving voters what they want—it requires leaders genuinely to lead, which means engaging in objective analysis of public questions and then seeking to persuading voters of the appropriate course of action, even if that is unpopular. Yet in the main, current political leaders adopt safe policies which do not confront voters with difficult choices and which serve their primary objective, which is retention of power. This is the antithesis of the examples set by Gorbachev and De Klerk who led societies which would have failed in the absence of radical change, where the risk of such failure was very high and where both leaders took a gamble in proposing change that would strip power from the social groups upon whom they relied for support. Such leadership is unknown in current conditions, yet ironically in many countries, including the United Kingdom,[36] the USA[37] and Australia,[38] voters crave political leadership which will make hard choices instead of prioritising self-interest.

6.4 The Obligation of Political Leaders to Promote Knowledge of Civics and Citizenship

Given the capacity of politicians to shape public opinion, they arguably have a special responsibility to ensure the flourishing of good citizenship. This goes beyond creating education programmes of the type discussed in Chap. 3, fundamental as that is, and involves using their influence to encourage citizens to become both informed and critical. Unfortunately, many politicians see an informed citizenry as a threat rather than as an asset. As discussed in Chap. 2 the reasons for this are obvious: Populist politicians, who are nowadays increasingly prominent, rely on attracting support by eliciting an emotional reaction in voters rather than by engaging in reasoned argument. Reasoned analysis is precisely what many politicians do not want from voters, particularly in instances where the policies they are advocating would be shown to be flawed if subject to informed scrutiny.

[36] Otte (2025).

[37] Sethi (2024).

[38] Knight (2025).

Arguably worse than taking advantage of civic ill-informedness is active promotion of it. An example of this is provided by the record of a 2006 inquiry by the Australian parliament's Joint Standing Committee on Electoral Matters into the state of civics education in Australia. The author appeared as a witness and had this interchange with Senator George Brandis, who subsequently became Attorney-General[39]:

Senator BRANDIS	When we talk about our system and the Constitution I do not think we should necessarily be teaching students—unless they are law students—about the particular provisions of the Constitution; what we should be teaching them about is democracy. It is in the high concept of democracy, rather than in the prosaic words of the Constitution, that we are going to capture people's imaginations.
Dr. Harris	I agree that you have to inspire in the students an appreciation of democracy, but their next question will be: how is this theory implemented in Australia? The answer is: through the mechanism of the Constitution. Then they will ask: how does the Constitution work and does it actually deliver what you say it promises?
Senator BRANDIS	Do you think they do say that? Or do they—because, with all its limitations, I think we all have a sense that Australia is a pretty well-functioning democracy— merely accept that, without requiring the statutory verification of it?............
Dr. Harris	They do accept that, but they are unconcerned with the defects of it—for example, the idea that you can win a general election with significantly fewer popular votes than the opposition. They do not think that far ahead, unless you point it out to them, because the Constitution conceals that possibility.
Senator BRANDIS	I know that has happened a couple of times but that can happen in the most sophisticated democracy, can't it?
Dr. Harris	The risk of it happening if you have proportional representation is very, very small. I was in New Zealand when they introduced the MMP system. At least you knew then that whatever government was formed had a majority of voters behind it. I think we should want our students and young people to ask those questions, and to say: 'This is a wonderful theory you are teaching us. Now show us how it works in the document.'
Senator BRANDIS	That is where I do not agree with you because, apart from teaching law students and perhaps politics students, I would not have thought you need to make the language of the document itself accessible to teach students, particularly secondary students, about the way Australian democracy works.

[39] Parliament of Australia (2006, pp. 39–40).

Dr. Harris But isn't it their Constitution?
Senator BRANDIS I am not saying you should not, but I do not think you need to.

How can it be said that students should not only be denied the tools to critique the constitution but not even be taught what it says? Blind acceptance that 'we all have a sense that Australia is a pretty well-functioning democracy' is surely an inadequate foundation upon which to build the ability to function as a citizen, but it encapsulates the approach of a representative of one of the parties that operates the duopoly that controls politics in Australia. Australia's constitution needs thoroughgoing reform to address multiple shortcomings, including the lack of a bill of rights, inadequate parliamentary scrutiny of the executive, an inefficient federal system, lack of autonomy for Indigenous peoples, reliance on convention rather than on law for the operation of key aspects of the constitution and the vesting of headship of state in a foreign monarch.[40] Most of these changes would lead to consequences which would be politically adverse to the parties that currently dominate politics in Australia, so it comes as no surprise that one of their leaders would be averse to people learning how the constitution works and thereby being exposed to its deficiencies. From their perspective, it is far preferable to have a citizen body who is unquestioning and accepts the platitude that Australia is a 'pretty well-functioning democracy.'

Blatant discouragement of voters becoming informed as a method of thwarting constitutional change were evident during the two most recent referenda on constitutional amendment in Australia. The first of these, held in 1999, was on the question of whether Australia should sever its link with the crown of the United Kingdom and become a republic.[41] Central to the debate was an understanding of the conventions governing the Governor-General's exercise of power on behalf of the monarch and whether these would apply to a president. Given the low level of civic knowledge in Australia, many voters simply did not understand the issues involved[42] and, like anyone faced with the question of whether to change a machine the workings of which they did not understand, were predisposed to vote No. It is for this reason that the slogan 'If you don't know, vote no'[43] used by the No campaign was so effective in defeating the proposal. What is significant about this is that the No campaign argument found it more profitable to focus not on the substantive constitutional issues, but rather on voters' lack of knowledge of them, actively discouraging them from informing themselves and actively encouraging them to retreat into negativity. The slogan embodied the absolute antithesis of good citizenship – indeed it is difficult to think of an exhortation more subversive of that value.

The second referendum, held in 2023, was on the question of whether the constitution should be amended so as to establish a body called the Voice to Parliament, which would be elected by Indigenous people to make representations to the government on matters affecting them.[44] Politicians opposed to the proposal said that it would

---

[40] For a full discussion of these issues see Harris (2020).

[41] Harris (2020, pp. 199–211).

[42] Higley and McAllister (2002, pp. 852, 854, 858–9).

[43] Australian Electoral Commission (1999, p. 9).

[44] Harris (2023a, b, pp. 227–50).

establish apartheid in Australia.[45] Anyone conversant with the racist character of the apartheid system, or that post-apartheid South Africa has a House of Traditional Leaders that performs the same role as the body proposed for Australia, could not possibly have accepted the bizarre proposition that a proposal to enhance the position of Australia's Indigenous peoples was analogous to apartheid. The point, however, is that few people had the background information needed to see the falsity of the argument. Similarly, the No campaign propagated the argument that the proposed amendment would require that the government accept representations made by the Voice—yet nothing in the text supported that conclusion. Logic also indicated that the Voice's representations could not possibly be binding: Any person or entity is entitled to make representations on policy to parliament or the government by contacting ministers, MPs and senators or appearing before parliamentary committees—but that does not mean that they have a right to challenge the lawfulness of that policy if their representations are not followed. To state otherwise would mean that every person who had lobbied the government and whose views were not taken into account when a policy was formulated would be able to initiate legal action challenging the policy, a proposition which would create an insoluble problem given that on every issue the government receives a multitude of conflicting representations from a variety of parties. Yet even this obvious point escaped voters in circumstances where, in the week the referendum was held, many did not know what the referendum was about, despite the fact that the campaign had lasted for 10 months.[46] This created an environment conducive to voters believing claims which, from the perspective of constitutional doctrine, were manifestly false. The pernicious slogan 'If you don't know, vote no' was once again used to ensure that the referendum proposal was rejected,[47] and contrasted unfavourably with the civic-minded counter-slogan used by one of the Indigenous bodies supporting the proposed amendment: 'If you don't know, find out!'.[48]

A political actor committed to good citizenship would want voters to maximise their understanding of the issues and to consider all points of view—even if that leads voters ultimately to vote in a way adverse to that political actor's own position. Such an attitude would also reflect a belief that a well-informed citizenry is likely to elect leaders of better quality, which will in turn lead to better government. Conversely, a political actor who encourages citizen ignorance not only signals a lack of confidence in their own position—because they do not want it to be subject to scrutiny—but also indicates a preference for voters being easily manipulated, unlikely to engage in analysis and therefore less likely carefully to evaluate the quality of those standing for office. A strategy founded on fostering civic ignorance represents the ultimate in subordination of the public interest to political gain.

Given their low level of civics knowledge, voters in Australia are particularly vulnerable to manipulation when confronted with a constitutional reform. Lack of

---

[45] Butler (2023), Bogle et al. (2023).

[46] Rachwani (2023).

[47] Manns (2023).

[48] Strathearn (2023).

knowledge also predisposes them against approving constitutional amendments. Yet, as the results of the survey discussed in Chap. 3 show, voters are amenable to constitutional change proposals—if provided with neutral information about their effect. The problem, as indicated by the 1999 and 2023 referendum campaigns, is that there is no shortage of political actors who are willing to propagate disinformation and who see neutral information as inimical to their interests. Speaking of the 2023 referendum, Labor Senator Jana Stewart said that it was said it was 'unfortunate' that millions of Australians 'went into the polling booths with fear instead of facts,' accusing opponents of the Voice of using 'Trumpian-style mis- and disinformation' against 'some of the most marginalised and disenfranchised communities.'[49]

As a proposed solution to this problem, there has in recent years been debate over whether 'truth in political advertising' legislation, imposing either a criminal or civil penalty for the making of factually misleading statements during elections, should be enacted. Polling in the wake of the 2023 referendum indicated that the introduction of such legislation was supported by 87% of respondents.[50] A bill was introduced into the Australian parliament in 2025 which would empower an Electoral Communications Panel to investigate statements of fact in election campaign material that were allegedly misleading or deceptive, and to impose a civil penalty for breaches. It would also have the power to require parties to cease publishing material found to be misleading or deceptive and to publish a retraction.[51] The bill mirrors similar truth in political advertising legislation in force in South Australia[52] and the ACT.[53]

The problem with such legislation is that it substitutes truth-finding by the voter—which lies at the core of the voter's role—with a declaration of truth by an organ of the state. As discussed in Chap. 2, tolerance—including tolerance of that which is false—is not only a practice required for good citizenship but is also a *sine qua non* of truth-finding. To repeat John Stuart Mill's celebrated defence of freedom of expression[54]

> ..the opinion which it is attempted to suppress by authority may possibly be true. Those who desire to oppress it, of course deny its truth; but they are not infallible. They have no authority to decide the question for all mankind, and exclude every other person from the means of judging. To refuse a hearing to an opinion because they are sure that it is false, is to assume that their certainty is the same thing as absolute certainty. All silencing of discussion is an assumption of infallibility.

According to this theory, because it is always *possible* that truths discovered by human reason are in fact errors which, if one is allowed to challenge them, may be replaced by a new truth,[55] one can never say *conclusively* that one has attained truth. All one can say is that rational argument, in which all voices are heard, maximises

[49] Karp (2023).

[50] Karp (2023).

[51] *Electoral Legislation Amendment (Electoral Communications) Bill 2025.*

[52] Section 113 *Electoral Act 1985* (SA).

[53] Section 297A *Electoral Act 1992* (ACT).

[54] Mill (1859, p. 37).

[55] Schauer (1982, pp. 24–9).

the chances of discovering truth. Mill also was of the view that falsity has a role in promoting truth, stating that[56]

> The peculiar evil of silencing the expression of an opinion is, that it is robbing the human race; posterity as well as the existing generation; those who dissent from the opinion, still more than those who hold it. If the opinion is right, they are deprived of the opportunity of exchanging error for truth: if wrong, they lose, what is almost as great a benefit, the clearer perception and livelier impression of truth, produced by its collision with error.

Determination of which of the competing facts a voter is confronted by is an inescapable burden of citizenship, which cannot be exercised on the citizen's behalf by the state. This was eloquently stated by Kennedy J in the United States Supreme Court decision in *United States v Alvarez*[57] as follows

> Permitting the government to decree this speech to be a criminal offense, whether shouted from the rooftops or made in a barely audible whisper, would endorse government authority to compile a list of subjects about which false statements are punishable. That governmental power has no clear limiting principle. Our constitutional tradition stands against the idea that we need Oceania's Ministry of Truth

Kennedy J also stated that[58]

> the response to the unreasoned is the rational; to the uninformed, the enlightened; to the straight-out lie, the simple truth.

The presumption that the citizen is deemed capable of distinguishing truth from falsehood lies at the foundation of democracy. Even if defects in civics education mean that that presumption is untrue, the principle that it is the citizen's role—indeed inescapable burden—to engage in political decision-making cannot be abandoned, least of all by vesting the state with the power to determine what is true and untrue. The remedy for citizen ill-preparedness to assume their role is not to proscribe expression but rather to implement education policies that will ensure that they are equipped with the intellectual tools they need to distinguish between truth and lies and to understand the values underlying good citizenship.

6.5 Good Citizenship and the Limits of the Law

A fact that the discussion of citizenship in the preceding chapters of this book reveals is that one ultimately comes to recognise the limits of the law in ensuring the flourishing of good citizenship. Law, and in particular constitutions, can take one part-way way along the path by explicitly incorporating dignity as a value in terms of which the constitution must be interpreted, by ensuring that rights are protected, that the electoral system provides for fair representation and that there are mechanisms by

---

[56] Mill (1859, p. 37).

[57] 567 US 709 (2012) 15–16.

[58] 567 US 709 (2012) 11.

which adequate scrutiny can be applied to government. However, the legal system concerns the way law is made, the rights and duties it creates and the remedies it provides for breach. It is therefore a coercive system and also an *ex post facto* one which is called upon only once a law has been contravened. In other words, the law does not make people good—it simply provides a remedy once they have infringed a rule. It also does not address the problem of behaviour which is unethical as distinct from being illegal. Of course, one hopes that the law has a deterrent effect that creates a disincentive to engage in wrongdoing, but surely instilling attitudes which reduce the impulse to break the law in the first place would address the problem of unlawful or unethical behaviour at a deeper level?

Good citizenship ultimately relies on voluntary behaviour guided by ethical concern for one's fellow human beings.[59] Voters and their leaders cannot be mandated to practise the civic virtues of reason, tolerance, participation and kindness—these values must become 'dispositions internalized within one's character.'[60] That can be achieved only through the cultivation of good citizenship and civic knowledge through education. In an age of a decrease in trust in democracy, and an increase in alienation and disconnection from politics, the need for that education becomes all the more pressing.

References

Addison P (2006) Churchill: the unexpected hero. Oxford University Press, Oxford

Anderson S (2016) Peter Dutton suggests Fraser government made mistake by resettling Lebanese refugees. ABC News. Accessed 22 Nov 2016

Australian Electoral Commission (1999) Yes/No referendum 1999 - Your official referendum pamphlet. (Australian Electoral Commission, Canberra)

Australian Public Service Commission (2023) Trust and satisfaction in Australian democracy – 2023 National Survey. Australian Public Service Commission, Canberra

Bogle A, Nguyen K, Workman M (2023) Pauline Hanson's One Nation may lose website names registered ahead of Indigenous Voice referendum campaign. The Guardian. Accessed 10 Aug 2022

Brennan M (2024) Economy, immigration, abortion, democracy driving voters. Gallup. Accessed 1 Nov 2024

Bufacchi V (2023) Why Cicero matters. Bloomsbury, London

Burke E (1777) The political tracts and speeches: of Edmund Burke, Esq. Member of Parliament for the city of Bristol. William Wilson, Dublin

Bustillo X, Bernstein A (2024) Former President Trump is found guilty in historic New York criminal case. NPR. Accessed 30 May 2024

Butler J (2023) Liberals accused of flirting with 'far-right fringe' after Sky News Australia show where Indigenous voice compared to apartheid. The Guardian. Accessed 2 May 2023

Cabral S (2021) Capitol riots: did Trump's words at rally incite violence? BBC News. Accessed 14 Feb 2021

Cameron S, McAllister I (2022) Trends in Australian political opinion - results from the Australian election study 1987–2022. Australian National University, Canberra

[59] Skach (2024, pp. 38–9).

[60] Peterson (2011 p. 134).

Cleal O (2024) There are now 27 women who have accused Donald Trump of sexual misconduct. Women's Agenda. Accessed 27 Oct 2024
Cox L (2018) The bullying and harassment of house of commons staff – independent inquiry report. House of Commons, London
Curtice J, Montagu I, Sivathasan C (2024) Damaged politics? The impact of the 2019–24 Parliament on political trust and confidence. National Centre for Social Research, London
Francis S (2022) Suella Braverman back as home secretary after resigning. BBC News. Accessed 26 Oct 2022
Galeotti M (1997) Gorbachev and his revolution. Macmillan, Houndmills
Gilbert M (1981) Churchill's political philosophy. Oxford University Press, Oxford
Gilomee H (2013) The last Afrikaner leaders: a supreme test of power. University of Virginia Press, Charlottesville
Grierson J (2021) Lies, damned lies: the full list of accusations against Boris Johnson. The Guardian. Accessed 11 Dec 2021
Hall B (2017) Lawyers representing asylum seekers are 'un-Australian': Peter Dutton. The Sydney Morning Herald. 28 August 2017
Harris B (2020) Constitutional reform as a remedy for political disenchantment in Australia – the discussion we need. Springer, Singapore
Harris B (2023a) The sports grants scandal: constitutional protection of socioeconomic rights as a remedy for Porkbarrelling. James Cook Univ Law Rev 29:43–70
Harris B (2023b) Indigenous peoples and constitutional reform in Australia. Springer, Singapore
Higley J and McAllister I (2002) Elite division and voter confusion: Australia's republic referendum in 1999. European Journal of Political Research 41:845–861
House of Commons Committee of Privileges (2023) Matter referred on 21 April 2022 (conduct of Rt Hon Boris Johnson) Final Report – Fifth Report of Session 2022–23. House of Commons, London
Ipsos (2024) Populism in 2024 – populism, anti-elitism and nativism 28-country Ipsos global advisor survey. Ipsos, North Sydney
Karp P (2018) Peter Dutton says Victorians scared to go out because of 'African gang violence.' The Guardian. Accessed 3 Jan 2018
Karp P (2023) Almost nine in 10 Australians support plan to outlaw lies in political advertising, poll shows. The Guardian. Accessed 19 Oct 2023
Knight B (2025) Days out from the federal election, this is what voters are telling Your Say. ABC News. Accessed 1 May 2025
Otte J (2025) We need real change, not fiddling at the edges': voters on Labour's first year. The Guardian. Accessed 7 July 2025
Parliament of Australia (2006) Joint standing committee on electoral matters - inquiry into civics and electoral education. Transcript of proceedings. Parliament of Australia, Canberra. Accessed 11 Aug 2006
Peterson A (2011) Civic republicanism and civic education: the education of citizens. Palgrave Macmillan UK, Houndmills
Luce E (2024) As scandals mount, the US loses its shame. Financial Times. Accessed 28 Oct 2024
Manns H (2023) Voice referendum: "If you don't know, vote no" – an old slogan for modern politics. Monash University. Accessed 24 Oct 2023
Marien S, Hooge M (2011) Does political trust matter? An empirical investigation into the relation between political trust and support for law compliance. Eur J Political Res 50:267–91
McGreal C, Pengelly M (2023) Jury finds Donald Trump sexually abused columnist E Jean Carroll. The Guardian. Accessed 10 May 2023
Mill JS (1859) On liberty. Gray J, Smith G (eds) (1991). Routledge, London
Mitchell A (2025) Bullying claims in parliament soared by 40% last year, watchdog reveals. The Independent. Accessed 24 June 2025.
Murphy (2018) Kelly O'Dwyer says MPs were bullied during spill, as senator vows to names. The Guardian. Accessed 4 Sept 2018

Peterson A (2011) Civic republicanism and civic education: the education of citizen. Palgrave Macmillan UK, Houndmills
Rachwani M (2023) 'I don't know what it's about': not enough done to explain the voice referendum, people in western Sydney say. The Guardian. Accessed 5 Oct 2023
Rosentiel T (2025) Americans across political spectrum share deep distrust & pessimism. National Opinion Research Centre, Chicago
Roy Morgan (2025) Top 10 issues shaping the 2025 federal election: cost of living and crime on the rise, climate change fades. Roy Morgan. Accessed 23 Jan 2025
Royal Commission into the Robodebt Scheme (2023) Report of the Royal Commission into the Robodebt Scheme. Commonwealth Government, Canberra
Schauer F (1982) Free speech: a philosophical inquiry. Cambridge University Press, Cambridge
Sethi A (2024) US voters want change, Biden's exit hasn't fixed that. Open Democracy. Accessed 23 July 2024
Skach C (2024) How to be a citizen - learning to rely less on rules and more on each other. Bloomsbury Publishing, London
Smith M (2024) General election 2024: what are the most important issues for voters? YouGov. Accessed 2 June 2024
Strathearn P (2023) 'If you don't know, find out', urge Voice campaigners in Murray Bridge. Murray Bridge News. Accessed 20 Sept 2023
Sullivan S (2021) Trump's phone call to Brad Raffensperger: six key points. The Guardian. Accessed 6 Jan 2021
Timm J (2016) Trump on hot mic: 'When You're a Star ... You Can Do Anything' to women. NBC News. Accessed 8 Oct 2016

Index

B. Harris, *Cultivating Good Citizenship*,
SpringerBriefs in Law, https://doi.org/10.1007/978-981-92-2740-2

MIX
Papier aus verantwortungsvollen Quellen
Paper from responsible sources
FSC® C105338

If you have any concerns about our products,
you can contact us on
ProductSafety@springernature.com

In case Publisher is established outside the EU,
the EU authorized representative is:
Springer Nature Customer Service Center GmbH
Europaplatz 3, 69115 Heidelberg, Germany

Printed by Libri Plureos GmbH
in Hamburg, Germany